a
positive
plan
for creating
more calm,
less *stress*

KAROL LADD

W PUBLISHING GROUP
A Division of Thomas Nelson Publishers
Since 1798

www.wpublishinggroup.com

A Positive Plan for Creating More Calm, Less Stress

Published by W Publishing Group, a Division of Thomas Nelson, Inc., P.O. Box 141000, Nashville, Tennessee 37214.

W Publishing Group books may be purchased in bulk for educational, business, fundraising, or sales promotional use. For information, please e-mail SpecialMarkets@ThomasNelson.com.

All Scripture quotations, unless otherwise indicated, are taken from The Holy Bible, New Century Version (NCV), copyright © 1987, 1988, 1991 by Word Publishing, a Division of Thomas Nelson, Inc. Used by permission.

Other Scripture references are from the following sources:

The King James Version of the Bible (KJV).

The Holy Bible, New International Version (NIV). Copyright © 1973, 1978, 1984, International Bible Society. Used by permission of Zondervan Bible Publishers.

The New King James Version (NKJV®), copyright © 1979, 1980, 1982, Thomas Nelson, Inc., Publishers.

The Holy Bible, New Living Translation (NLT), copyright © 1996. Used by permission of Tyndale House Publishers, Inc., Wheaton, Illinois 60189. All rights reserved.

New American Standard Bible (NASB), copyright © 1960, 1977, 1995 by The Lockman Foundation.

Quotations designated (NET) are from The NET Bible®, copyright © 2003 by Biblical Studies Press, L.L.C., www.netbible.com. All rights reserved. Scripture quoted by permission.

Library of Congress Cataloging-in-Publication Data

Ladd, Karol.
    A positive plan for creating more calm, less stress / by Karol Ladd.
      p. cm.
Includes bibliographical references.
    ISBN 0-8499-0616-4
    1. Home economics. 2. Women—Time management. 3. Women—Religious life. 4. Home—Religious aspects—Christianity. I. Title.
    TX147.L324 2005
    640—dc22

    2004029472

Printed in the United States of America

05 06 07 08 09 RRD 9 8 7 6 5 4 3 2

Contents

Step Four:
Roll with the Punches

Step Five:
Strengthen Family Relationships

Too Blessed to Be Stressed?

*You will never be the person you can be if pressure,
tension, and discipline are taken out of your life.*

DR. JAMES G. BILKEY

*I have told you these things, so that in me you may have
peace. In this world you will have trouble. But take heart! I
have overcome the world.*

JOHN 16:33 NIV

What would a stress-free day look like in your life? Picture this:

- No complaining, whining, or arguing from the kids
- No errands to run
- No responsibilities, deadlines, or forms to fill out
- No piles of stuff to sift through
- No phone calls to return
- No physical aches or pains
- No unexpected challenges
- No grocery shopping or cooking
- No complaining, whining, or arguing from your hubby

Oh, wouldn't it be lovely? Let's face it: The only person who has a stress-free day is the one who isn't breathing anymore! All the rest of us living, breathing women face daily struggles and responsibilities that tend to chip away at the calm and peace in our lives. Notice this book is not titled *A Positive Plan for Creating Total Calm and No Stress*. I wish I could tell you differently, but the truth is there will always be a certain amount of stress in our lives. The good news is we can learn to diminish its effect and increase our capacity for calm both in our homes and in our hearts. That's what this book is all about.

Certainly our lives are filled with the joys and blessings of motherhood. We love our families. We are thankful for them, but we may not always be thankful for the tensions that family life brings. No doubt each of us could use a positive plan to smooth over the rough edges and make our homes havens for everyone to enjoy.

Here's the Plan

Most likely you are reading this book because you want to build your home in a positive way. You sincerely desire more calm in your life. Me too. That's why I've written this book. I'm all about being practical. There are enough books on my shelf that give me pie-in-the-sky ideas; I want something that gives me a real-life handle on maintaining calm in the daily trenches of motherhood.

In my own life, I have learned that I work best with a plan of action. Give me the steps, and I'll carry them out. You will notice that this book is broken down into five significant steps designed to move you toward more calm in your life. They are not laid out in a particular order. You can go to step 4 ("Roll with the Punches") first if you think that section would meet an immediate need. Later you can go back to steps 1 through 3.

I've always said, "The best way to eat an elephant is one bite at a time." Creating more calm and less stress in your life may seem like an elephant-sized task. Don't bite off more than you can chew! Progressively work through the simple steps in this book one at a time. Ask God to guide and direct you. Before long you'll find yourself moving step by step, bite by bite, toward more calm and less stress in your home and in your life.

You may want to join together with friends and read through the book as a group. At the end of each chapter you will find a section called "Calming Thoughts," which gives you a scripture to read, a sample prayer to pray, and some introspective questions to ask. This section is great not only for personal growth, but also for facilitating group Bible study and small group discussions.

My Gift to You

It is my hope that this book will give you a dose of encouragement as well as a practical plan for peace—whatever your circumstances. You may be a mother of preschoolers, a mother of teens, or an empty nester. You may have an additional job (part-time, full-time, or volunteer) outside the home. You may home-school your kids. You may be a mother of one or a mother of many. But wherever you are on your journey of motherhood, your desire is the same as every woman's: to pull together the loose ends, reduce stress, and experience more calm in your daily life.

I wish I could come to your home and sweep away all the stressors and challenges you face, but alas, that's not possible. What I can do is give you the gift of this book. I'm not coming to you as Mrs. Have-It-All-Together. I'm coming as a fellow struggler who, like you, is searching for the best plan for experiencing more calm and less stress in my own family.

So where did I find the solutions I present in the coming chapters? First, from the treasure trove of God's Truth. That's the foundation of this book. God made us, and I'm convinced He offers us the best plan for experiencing a joy-filled life. The Bible, His Word to us, is rich with passages about peace, calm, and wisdom for living. I share many of these passages in the pages that follow.

I also believe there is wisdom in many counselors. As you will see, I have sought out experts in different key areas (such as home organization, discipline, diets, and relationships) to give us pointers, tips, and information to help us in our growth. Last, I have added a delicious topping of hope, strength, and joy from yours truly, "The Positive Lady" (as I'm affectionately known in some circles). And there you have it: a complete package designed to give you just the boost of blessing that you need!

Go ahead—take your first step toward more calm and less stress in your life. I'm walking right alongside you through the pages of this book. More importantly, the God of peace is with you always. He is your strength for the journey.

1

Divine Delights
in a Less-Than-Perfect Family

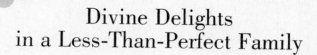

Our home joys are the most delightful earth affords, and the joy of parents in their children is the most holy joy of humanity. It makes their hearts pure and good; it lifts men up to their Father in heaven.

JOHANN HEINRICH PESTALOZZI

Take delight in the LORD,
  and he will give you your heart's desires.
Commit everything you do to the LORD.
  Trust him, and he will help you.

PSALM 37:4–5 NLT

As a former science teacher and a current mom, I've discovered that the laws of family physics are relatively similar to some of the natural laws of physics. For example:

1. An object at rest (such as a teenager or husband or family dog) tends to stay at rest, unless otherwise motivated by a phone call, persistent nagging, or a biscuit.
2. An object in motion (such as a mouth) tends to stay in

motion, especially when grumbling, complaining, or eating.

3. For every action (push, shove, or negative comment), there is an equal and opposite reaction, until a parent steps in and breaks it up.

4. Laundry spontaneously tends to flow from being concentrated within one location to becoming diffused or dispersed to various regions of the house.

5. The increase in the amount of activities on the family calendar is equal to the tension and friction added to the system, minus the communication achieved within the system.

Talk about theories of relativity! Family relationships require a great deal of energy, without a doubt. But our goal as mothers is not to create a utopia with seamless interactions and continual bliss in the home. Our goal is to delight in the family God has given us and work through family challenges in positive ways. Then our homes can be havens where family members find encouragement and strength to become all that God has created them to be.

As moms, we are the ones who tend to set the tone for our homes. *Now wait a minute,* you may be thinking. *We're only human! We struggle with feelings, emotions, fatigue, and stress, just like the rest of our family members.* That's true. But like it or not, we have a high calling: to influence and maintain the positive atmosphere in our homes. That's part of our role as mothers. I guess you could say we are the "Positive Attitude Coordinators."

Solomon put it this way: "A wise woman strengthens her family, but a foolish woman destroys hers by what she does."[1] The fact is our words, actions, and attitudes permeate our homes and have a profound effect upon our families. We can choose to be refreshing delights, or we can choose to be contentious complainers. I don't know about you, but I would rather build my home with delight than destroy it with discouragement. At least that's my intention. It's not easy! The road to delight takes determination. Won't you join me as we begin to step in the right direction?

Our Unique Road to Delight

Do you ever look at other families and secretly think to yourself, *How do they do it?* They always love and support one another. Their kids are high achievers and stellar students. They seem to do everything well, and do it with a smile. As you watch them, little feelings of jealousy, envy, or guilt creep in and begin destroying your confidence as a mom. Been there?

Then there are those families that make you shake your head and think to yourself, *I can't believe the way they parent their kids. I would never do what they are doing.* Tiny tidbits of pride begin to seep in as you secretly thank God that your family is not like them. Been there?

Comparisons and assumptions are common to all of us. It makes sense to try to gauge our success by looking at others and observing how they do things. Businesses do it; athletes do it; even churches do it. We all tend to compare our success (or failure) by the meter and measure of others. But that's not how it should be between families.

Although it goes against our natural grain, we must redirect our thinking away from comparisons with other families. On the road to delight, we need to picture a big sign that says, "Thou shalt not compare." God has given each family a different mix of people and personalities. No two families are exactly the same.

Recently I heard a story about identical twin sisters who married identical twin brothers. (The two sets of twins met at a twins convention, of all places!) At the time of the story, the couples lived next door to each other. With two sets of identical parents, you would think that their families would be, well, identical. They're not. In fact, their families are very different. They have different looks and different personalities, different interests and different talents. They are involved in different activities, and the two sets of parents discipline their children in different ways.

Now if two sets of identical twin parents do not have identical families, then why in the world would we think there is a family out there with whom we can compare ours? Each family (yours, mine, and others) is a unique blend of personalities, abilities, talents, handicaps, and idiosyncrasies. As parents, we bring into our families a variety of backgrounds, work ethics, political persuasions, and religious beliefs.

One of the greatest joys we can experience in motherhood is to delight in our God-given families without comparing them with others. Let's throw away the assumption that other families have it all together (or are a mess, for that matter). We don't know what goes on inside their homes. What we do know is that God has given each of us a unique group of family members. Our delight comes in following God's purpose and plan for our own families, not someone else's.

Learning to Delight

As we journey down different paths, we must learn to embrace the portions that God has given us. I say "learn" because it's not an easy task. Ours may not be the perfect, loving families we always pictured. Our circumstances may not correspond with those best-laid plans we plotted in our minds as young women. So how do we delight in both the good and the bad of our lives?

The Apostle Paul put it this way: "I have learned to be satisfied with the things I have and with everything that happens. I know how to live when I am poor, and I know how to live when I have plenty. I have learned the secret of being happy [or content] at any time in everything that happens . . . I can do all things through Christ, because he gives me strength."[2]

Perhaps you've heard that last sentence put another way: "I can do all things through Christ who strengthens me." It's a well-loved, oft-used Bible quote. But did you realize the words are referring to the power God gives us to be content in our circumstances? Paul is saying that he has learned (there's that word *learn*) the secret to being happy, and it doesn't rest in having all the best that life has to offer. It doesn't rest in circumstances. The secret is found in Christ—Christ, who gives us strength for the journey.

We can learn to be content in our personal lives as moms by recognizing that we don't have all of the strength, wisdom, and ability we need to handle motherhood on our own. We need help from above. Turning to God, we can say, "Lord, help me to have patience, because I don't have it within myself to be patient right now." Or, "Father, please give me strength for today. I'm so tired, and yet I have so much to do."

Although we may be weak, our loving Heavenly Father is strong. He is able to give us wisdom when we discipline our kids, grace when we deal with our family members, and kindness when we speak to others. Learning to be content in our circumstances and with the people around us doesn't mean being complacent. It doesn't mean ignoring problems or pretending that everything's all right when it's not. It means learning to rely day by day on the true source of our strength: Christ Himself.

Choosing Delight

We can learn to keep our eyes on Christ and look to Him for help—or we can choose to focus on our circumstances and become overwhelmed. It's a day-by-day, moment-by-moment choice. I love the way my friend Rachel finds humor in the ups and downs of motherhood. The following is an excerpt from her book, *Wake Up Laughing*. She gives us a perspective of hope and delight in the midst of disillusionment and despair:

Before my first child was born, I remember older, wiser women saying things like, "Enjoy the time you have to yourself before the baby comes!"

At the time, I wasn't thrilled with the time on my hands due to the weight on my bod and the anticipations of seeing the baby in person. I couldn't wait to play dress-up with my real live baby doll. Diaper and formula commercials sent me into La La Land, daydreaming about holding my bundle of joy. I especially liked the ones in which a buff-bodied daddy peeks into Junior's crib in the middle of the night, picks up a porcelain-skinned baby, and nuzzles him. (Notice how the babies are either sleeping or smiling in these propaganda pieces.) I know that's what I had in mind—a studly husband and a picture-perfect baby bonding at 2:00 a.m. in the Ralph Lauren designer nursery while I'm sawing logs in the next room.

But my daydream images became fuzzy with the arrival of baby and the relentless longing for a few hours of un-interrupted shut-eye. My cowardly friends who went before me to baby boot camp didn't clue me in to reality, and I wanted to wring their necks . . .

And what of hubby-turned-new-dad? Well, he discovered talents he never knew he had. He had the uncanny ability to sleep through our baby's cries. So while he sawed the logs I could only dream about, I cradled my gargantuan mammary glands in my arms and waddled down the hall to the Wal-Mart decorated nursery, bonding with Junior at 2:00 a.m. . . . and 3:00 a.m. . . . and 4:00 a.m. I did enough bonding that first year to be the prototype for human superglue.

And I would love to know where the television producers found that porcelain-skinned infant. I quickly became acquainted with the oxymoron "baby acne." My newborn would have been a shoo-in for a Clearasil commercial . . .

If you're a mom, I'm preaching to the parental choir. First comes love, then comes marriage, and on the heels of the baby carriage comes disillusionment. Of course, we do experience precious moments with our babies that we will forever hold dear. But on the whole, children are needy and can wreak havoc on your housekeeping, sleep quota, and love life.

When we're knee-deep in diapers, it's important to put things into perspective by reviewing two facts. Fact #1: This is an intense time of life. Fact #2: Babies grow up quickly, and as they do, things get easier . . . If you're a relatively new mom or know someone who is and have had a particularly exhausting day (or week or month!), ask God to help you put things in perspective. He may just help you see that beneath your exhaustion is still a heart brimming with grati-tude for the priceless, albeit tiring, gift of children.[3]

Perspective is everything! It's also a choice. Will we choose to see the humor, delight, and joy in life, or will we only look at the diffi-culties, frustrations, and failures? Teresa of Avila, a devout woman of God who lived in the sixteenth century, reminds us of the secret to divine delight each day:

Let nothing disturb thee,
Let nothing affright thee,
All things are passing,
God changeth never.[4]

We can choose to delight in the ups and downs of each stage of motherhood, recognizing that each stage lasts only a short period of time—but God never changes. If you feel overwhelmed right now, take heart. Things will get better. God has not left you.

A Psalm for the Slightly Unconventional Family

When I think about families portrayed in the Bible, I can't help but notice that every one of them qualified as less than perfect. One fam-ily in particular sticks out in my mind as a far-from-stellar example of family values and bonding. Oddly, the dad in this family is referred to in Scripture as "a man after God's own heart."[5] We know him as King David. Jesus Himself was part of his lineage. A brief glance through the Old Testament reminds us that David's family life included incest, adultery, murder, scandal, rejection, disloyalty, and heartache (among other things). Yet God in His abundant grace and eternal providence still used David's family in a mighty way, eventually bringing forth the Messiah through his descendants. His entries in the Book of Psalms speak powerfully to our hearts, especially as we see him looking to the Lord in the midst of his difficulties.

I want us to look in particular at Psalm 37.[6] Although this psalm was not written specifically about families, I think it applies in many ways to our journey as mothers and our role as Positive Attitude Coordinator in our homes.

David begins the psalm in the first verse by saying, "Don't worry about the wicked. Don't envy those who do wrong." In other words, we should keep our eyes on our own lives and families and not look at others with envy, comparison, or jealousy. Sound familiar? He goes on to say:

Trust in the LORD and do good.
   Then you will live safely in the land and prosper.
Take delight in the LORD,
   and he will give you your heart's desires.

Commit everything you do to the LORD.
   Trust him, and he will help you . . .

Be still in the presence of the LORD,
   and wait patiently for him to act.

In these verses, David encourages us to keep our eyes on God, not on people. We are to delight in the Lord. What does it mean to delight in someone? It means to find great joy or pleasure in who the person is, in being with him or her. Most of us delight (most of the time, anyway) in our kids and spouses, but what about the Lord? Do we find our joy in Him? If not, then we need to draw closer to Him. As we get to know Him through His Word, we can't help but take delight in such an awesome God.

Let's be clear, though. Receiving our "heart's desires" does not mean getting everything we want when we want it. It does mean that as we delight in the Lord, the number one desire of our hearts will become a desire to know Him better and to find our soul's pleasure in Him. That's a desire He will surely bring to pass. When it comes to knowing Him, God will not leave us wanting!

David also tells us, "Commit everything you do to the LORD." That means committing our families to Him. It means committing our attitudes to Him. It means entrusting and submitting everything in our lives to His control. Easy to do? Not at all. But it's easier when we're submitting to a God in whom we delight! And as we commit ourselves to Him, David says, He will help us.

We must be patient. In our fast-paced world, we want everything now. But God's work is not necessarily one of speed. In His time, in His way, and in His sovereign wisdom, He will act on our behalf. He will do what He intends to do in our lives—not on our timetable, but on His.

We're an impatient bunch, aren't we? Sometimes it's easy for me to become discouraged when I must discipline my daughters and teach them something I feel they should have already learned. I must be patient as God works in their lives through time and training—trusting that, slowly but surely, He is developing His character in them. He is doing the same in you and me.

I encourage you to read Psalm 37 in its entirety. But for our purposes right now, let's move ahead to verse 23: "The steps of the godly are directed by the LORD. He delights in every detail of their lives."

Stop and think about that for a moment. God delights in every detail of our lives! What are the details of *your* life? Do they include your relationships with family members? Yes. What about laundry, work, friendships, errands, homework, paying bills? Yes! It's amazing to think that the God of the universe delights in even the smallest details of our daily existence. Nothing is too small for Him!

Which leads us to verse 24: "Though they [His people] stumble, they will not fall, for the LORD holds them by the hand." As God's children, we stumble. We make mistakes, and we don't handle every situation the way we should. But that's no reason for despair. Why? Because God holds us by the hand! Get a visual picture of that in your mind. Just as we reach down and hold our precious children by the hand, helping them take their tiny, often stumbling steps, so God holds us. We are not alone in our role as mothers. God is with us, holding our hands as we hold our children's. We may stumble, but His grip is strong and sure. He will help us.

Seeing Clearly

Oh, may we delight in Him as He becomes the desire of our hearts! As we face the realities of our less-than-perfect families, may He be our divine delight! A fitting close for this chapter comes to us from a woman who could see clearly, despite the fact that she was physically blind. Born in 1820, Fanny Crosby saw God's grace and love throughout her life. Her physical sight was taken from her through improper medical treatment at the wee age of six months, yet her spiritual sight led her to see a spring of joy.

The story is told of a particular day when she desperately needed five dollars and didn't know where she could get it. As was her custom, she began praying about the matter. In just a few minutes, a stranger appeared at her door with just the right amount! "I have no way of accounting for this," she wrote, "except to believe that God, in answer to my prayer, put it into the heart of this good man to bring the money. My first thought was, it is so wonderful the way the

Lord leads me. I immediately wrote the poem, and Dr. Lowry set it to music."[7]

What poem? Perhaps you are familiar with Fanny Crosby's beloved hymn "All the Way My Savior Leads Me." It first appeared in a Sunday-school collection entitled *Brightest and Best*, compiled by William H. Doane and Fanny's composer, Robert Lowry, in 1875. I believe the second verse of this hymn speaks directly to us as we embrace our role as Positive Attitude Coordinators in our homes and seek divine delight on our journey down the road of motherhood:

> All the way my Savior leads me
> Cheers each winding path I tread
> Gives me grace for every trial
> Feeds me with the living bread
> Though my weary steps may falter
> And my soul athirst may be
> Gushing from the Rock before me
> Lo a spring of joy I see.

Calming Thoughts

Scripture Reading: Matthew 14:22–36, "Peter's Prayer"

Quiet Meditations:
- How would you describe Peter's faith in verses 28–29?
- Why do you think Peter started to sink? What was Jesus' response to Peter's prayer?
- When is the last time you cried out to God for help?

Personal Prayer:
O wonderful, loving, and holy Heavenly Father, I praise You for Your wisdom, power, and strength! I praise You for Your presence in my life! I confess I haven't always taken my needs and cares to You. I have often tried to solve my own problems. Teach me to rely on You as my strength. Thank You for Your tender care over the details of my life. Thank You for holding my hand and keeping me from falling. Mold me and make me into a positive influence in my home. Help me through the storms of life, and lead me down the path of contentment and divine delight. I want to find my spring of joy in You alone! In Jesus' name I pray, amen.

2

Confessions of an Overwhelmed Mom

Plenty of people miss their share of happiness,
not because they never found it,
but because they didn't stop to enjoy it.

W. FEATHER

The LORD is my shepherd;
  I have everything I need.
He lets me rest in green pastures.
  He leads me to calm water.
He gives me new strength.
  He leads me on paths that are right for the good of his
  name.

PSALM 23:1–3

Cashier: "Do you want your receipt in the bag?"

Me, with a perplexed look: "Ummm."

Cashier: "Receipt in the bag or in your purse, lady? It's really a simple question."

It's a little scary when I can't come up with answers to no-brainer questions. You can imagine what I'm like at the grocery store when I have to decide between paper or plastic, cash or credit. And don't even get me started on ordering a vanilla latte at Starbucks. (Tall, grande, or venti? Caf or decaf? Whipped cream or no?) It's enough to send me over the edge!

I affectionately refer to my inability to think clearly at times as "brain blips." Maybe a better term would be "mental overload."

How did I get to this disoriented state? The first rumblings of overwhelm began when I brought my first precious baby girl home from the hospital. Diapers, feeding, laundry, bath, more feeding, diapers, spit up, ear infection, laundry—it wasn't as easy as I thought it would be. Eventually I graduated from those early stages of being rattled and found my life returning to some semblance of order until . . . my second precious baby girl was born. Then I was back to caring for all the needs of a newborn—plus managing a toddler. The good news is, even those responsibilities eventually settled into a peaceful rhythm.

When my older daughter entered kindergarten, I thought my life would be smooth sailing from then on. I was wrong. My overwhelm increased one soccer game at a time. Allow me to explain. The year Grace (my older daughter) entered kindergarten, I joined the volunteer ranks of hundreds of moms cutting, pasting, and driving on school field trips. One of my newfound friends/volunteer moms informed me that she was starting a kids' soccer team, and she wanted to give me the opportunity to sign Grace up before all the spots were taken.

Soccer? I didn't know much about the game, except that everyone else was talking about it. Grace had never expressed an interest in soccer, but who was I to hold her back? Maybe she had the potential to make the women's Olympic soccer team one day, but how would she ever have that chance unless I started her at the age of five? Besides, I figured, going to soccer games would give me an opportunity to get to know the other moms. Practice every Tuesday during our normal dinnertime? *Well, I guess that's okay,* I thought to myself. *Just as long as it doesn't get in the way of church on Wednesdays and gymnastics on Thursdays.*

The next year my other daughter, Joy, joined a different soccer team with a different set of practice times. And as if that didn't require enough schedule juggling during the week, we now had two games to get to on Saturdays. As the girls grew older, their practices grew longer and more frequent. Did I mention we also added volleyball and basketball seasons to our year-round athletic cycle of practices and games?

Kindergarten and sports were only the beginning of the treadmill. Add homeroom-mom responsibilities, school meetings and programs, field trips, and luncheons. Mix in time with friends, exercise, housework, cooking, doctor appointments, dentist visits, helping with homework, and trips to the cleaners. Before I knew it, I was juggling more balls than I could dream of holding. Each one represented a good and worthwhile activity, but their sheer number was slowly pushing me into a frazzled state.

Why did I do it? Why did I add all these activities to my plate and my kids' plates? Some of them could not have been avoided (like doctor appointments); yet some certainly could have been circumvented, postponed, or never added at all. To be brutally honest with you, the root causes of my overscheduling were deep within my own heart: the fear of being left out or left behind, guilt that I wasn't doing enough for my kids, and pride that I was asked to be in charge. Comparing myself and my family with others played a big part in my overinvolvement too. I suspect I am not the only mom who has ever found herself in such a pickle!

In fact, as I was writing this chapter, a friend called me to say, "Pray for me. I feel overwhelmed with all of the things going on with each of my children. If I could just stay on top of it all, I would feel great, but I can't. There's simply too much. Then I hear about all the things other families are doing, and I feel guilty." All I could say was, "Honey, can I relate!" And we stopped and prayed.

If you have not yet stepped onto the fast-lane, activity-driven treadmill, don't do it! Save yourself before it's too late! As for the rest of us who are running on overload, we must find a way to get off, or at least to slow down. We must find practical solutions to overcome our overwhelmed state.

From Overwhelm to Under Him

We can start by taking a deliberate look at our lives and then considering what we can do to move ourselves and our families in a positive, more calming direction. "How's that working for you?" as Dr. Phil would say. We need to ask, *Has my pattern for life brought about the desired goals? Is my life better for the wear?* In my own life, the overload of activities only served to make me more stressed out and not so nice to the people around me. For my kids' part, they were burned out on soccer and gymnastics by age twelve.

So what can we do differently? Is it a matter of simply wiping all the activities off our calendars and getting rid of everything that stresses us out? That's a nice idea, but it's not practical. Over the years it has become evident to me that the most effective, realistic way to replace overwhelm with personal order and peace boils down to two basic elements:

1. Don't do everything; do the right things.
2. Rely on God, not yourself, for your strength.

How exactly do we know what the right things are? And how do we rely on God, when we're so used to relying on ourselves to get things done? Good questions. Let's examine both of the elements we just listed in the light of God's leadership in our lives.

Doing the Right Things

If God truly delights in the details of our lives (as we read in Psalm 37 in the last chapter), then He is thrilled for us to come to Him for direction on those details. In fact, throughout the Bible God encourages us, even implores us, to come to Him in prayer to ask for His help, His wisdom, and His guidance. In the New Testament we read, "But if any of you [overwhelmed moms] needs wisdom, you should ask God for it. He is generous and enjoys giving to all people, so he will give you wisdom."[1] (Of course, I added the part in brackets.)

Considering God's willingness to help us and direct us, perhaps we should try making decisions a new way: Before we say yes to an added activity or responsibility, let's first lay it before the Lord.

Have you ever thought about asking God whether your six-year-old daughter should play on the basketball team? I know I didn't. I just went ahead and signed her up, because everyone else was doing it. It seems crazy as I look back now. I did so many things just like a cow in a herd, aimlessly following all the other cows. (No offense to cows intended.) Oh, the frustrations I could have avoided if I had asked for God's direction in my family's life rather than following the crowd!

We should never hesitate to ask God for guidance. As we said in chapter 1, He loves us and wants to hold our hands to keep us from falling. David understood this. The Psalms include many of David's prayers seeking God's direction for his life. Perhaps his prayer in Psalm 5:8 can be ours too: "LORD, since I have many enemies, show me the right thing to do. Show me clearly how you want me to live."

We can personalize David's prayer by changing the word *enemies* to words that specify some of our own enemies—*distractions, activities, opportunities, good things.* Good things? That's right. Perhaps you've heard the axiom "Good is the enemy of best." Even good things can be the wrong things if they keep us from doing the right things. We're not supposed to be doing nothing in our lives, of course; but neither are we supposed to be doing a bunch of nice and good things. We're supposed to be following God and seeking His best and perfect path for us and our families. Maybe our prayer can be, "Lord, since I have so many good opportunities in front of me, show me the right thing to do. Show me clearly how You want me to live."

I'm reminded of Paul's words: "Everything you do or say should be done to obey Jesus your Lord. And in all you do, give thanks to God the Father through Jesus."[2] Think about running everything we choose to do through the sieve of this verse. When we have an opportunity to add something to our lives, we can ask ourselves, "Am I obeying the Lord by taking this on, and will I be able to carry it out with a thankful heart?"

We may not know the answers to these questions at first. That's why we need to seek God's direction and wisdom. I have found that as I seek God's guidance, He is faithful to show me the answers in one way or another—sometimes through a bit of information or advice from a wise friend, sometimes through a compelling nudge in my spirit. My problem quite often is I simply forget to ask! Instead I forge ahead on my own, never stopping to pray or to listen.

Solomon said, "The wise look ahead to see what is coming, but fools deceive themselves."[3] If we want to be wise women, we need to take a deliberate look at what we are doing and why we are doing it. It's easy to deceive ourselves into thinking that we can do it all. Sometimes we look at another woman and think, *She seems to handle everything so well. I should be able to do that too.* But we're deceived on two points: One, we don't know for sure if she's really handling everything well, since we don't know what's going on behind the scenes; and two, each of us is created differently. Some women can juggle many responsibilities with ease, while others cannot. Don't deceive yourself. Be the woman God created you to be, and do the things He is directing you to do. Say no to the rest.

Relying on God

Let's be careful not to assume that once we're doing the right things, everything will be smooth sailing. God doesn't promise we'll live the simple life when we're in the center of His will. If He did, then every prophet and saint in the Bible must have been doing the wrong things!

As we know, these people were (for the most part) doing the right things, but they experienced challenges. They also experienced God's strength in the midst of the challenges. We need to do the same.

Here's the question we need to ask ourselves: Are we going to rely on our own energy, perseverance, and know-how to make it through life, or are we going to look to God for strength? In my own experience, I have learned that my personal calm does not come from having perfectly tranquil circumstances. It comes from looking to the Lord for strength despite the circumstances and challenges that come my way.

No matter how well we plan and prayerfully choose only the right things to do, we will still have times when we feel rattled. We will still have disappointments and discouragements that will tend to pull us down or zap our strength. We must look beyond ourselves. We don't have all it takes to stand firm on our own. God will give us the strength we need. We may be weak, but He is strong.

We can find words of encouragement in the little Book of Habakkuk found in the Old Testament. In a few short pages, Habakkuk proclaims his trust in God even in the midst of fear and difficulties. He boldly declares his faith that even in the worst of situations, God will give him what he needs. Perhaps as you read his words you can relate to his anxious feelings, which are ultimately changed to a dependence on the Sovereign Lord:

> I trembled inside when I heard all this [referring to the powerful way God was going to deal with a wicked nation]; my lips quivered with fear. My legs gave way beneath me, and I shook in terror. I will wait quietly for the coming day when disaster will strike the people who invade us. Even though the fig trees have no blossoms, and there are no grapes on the vine; even though the olive crop fails, and the fields lie empty and barren; even though the flocks die in the fields, and the cattle barns are empty, yet I will rejoice in the LORD!

I will be joyful in the God of my salvation. The Sovereign LORD is my strength! He will make me as surefooted as a deer and bring me safely over the mountains.[4]

Although Habukkuk's fear threatened to overwhelm him, he chose to find his joy and strength in the God of his salvation. He chose to believe that God would replace his shaky legs with the surefootedness of a deer and bring him safely over the mountain of trouble that stood before him.

What is your mountain? Are your emotions getting the best of you? Do you have too much to do? Are some of the balls you're juggling starting to hit the ground? Habakkuk's words serve as a reminder to all of us to take our eyes off our circumstances and look instead to the Sovereign Lord who is our strength. God may not change our circumstances, but He can give us the surefootedness of a deer to help us make it over the mountain.

Over and over again in the Bible, God's message to His people was to be strong and courageous. Why? Because they had the strength and ability to handle the battles of life on their own? No! God told His people to be strong and courageous because He was with them. As they relied on Him, He would give them strength. I could choose many passages from the Old Testament that repeat this message, but one of my favorites is found in Isaiah. As you read these words from the Lord, think of them as a message to you as a mother:

> So don't worry, because I am with you.
>> Don't be afraid, because I am your God.
> I will make you strong and will help you;
>> I will support you with my right hand that saves you.[5]

Don't you find it comforting to know that God is with you? He doesn't want you to fret or to rely on your own resources. Certainly, as moms, we have responsibilities to fulfill; but in the midst of them, God wants us to find our strength and help in Him. Even the dynamic apostle Paul relied on the Lord and not himself. When he asked God to remove a particular physical challenge, God told him something we would all do well to remember: "My grace is enough for you. When you are weak, my power is made perfect in you."[6]

He Is Able

Are God's grace, power, and strength truly sufficient to meet all our needs? Often we don't give Him a chance to prove the answer, because we're not willing to change our focus or take the time to seek Him. Impatiently, we try to make it on our own; or we turn to a pacifier—a drink, a pill, a carton of Chunky Monkey, a shopping spree—rather than commit ourselves to the harder work of going to God.

I must make a brief side note here. I have become increasingly aware of the number of doctors doling out drugs to help women handle everything from overwhelm to anger. I understand there are times (like postpartum) or circumstances or physical reasons why some people may need anxiety medication, and I don't want to diminish that need. My concern, however, is that many women are going to medications first instead of going to the root of the problem.

Allow me to illustrate with something that is found in every yard that has green grass: weeds. Most of us are well aware that weeds must be pulled up by the roots; otherwise they will come back and invade our yards again. Nevertheless, most home improvement stores sell a wonderful tool called a weed-whacker. It's fun and easy to use, and it takes care of the tops of the weeds quickly. The problem is the weeds are not really gone; they're just temporarily whacked. The surface parts have been removed from sight, but the roots remain.

Often surface issues such as anxiety, moodiness, or depression can be delightfully whacked by medication. That doesn't get to the root of the problem, however. We need God's help and strength to effectively deal with the root causes of our struggles. Only then can we be done with them permanently. Please don't misunderstand me. Medication has its place, but it should never be used to sidestep the real issues. Like weed-whacking, taking a pill is quick and easy. Working through issues with God's help and strength, on the other hand, takes time, patience, and discipline.

Let's choose to go to God and find our healing in Him first. God may indeed lead us to seek the help of medication—but not as a substitute for working with Him to get to the root of our problems. Often we can't see our own needs and weaknesses. We can't see what's under the surface of our own hearts. That's why we need God's powerful, healing touch to convict us and renew us—to pull the weeds out by the roots. As David said, "God, examine me and know my heart; test me and know my nervous thoughts. See if there is any bad thing in me. Lead me on the road to everlasting."[7]

Are we willing to place ourselves in the hands of the Great Gardener? Jesus said, "I am the true vine; my Father is the gardener." He went on to explain, "I am the vine, and you are the branches. If any remain in me and I remain in them, they produce much fruit. But without me they can do nothing."[8] Are you seeing the picture of reliance that God desires for us? Apart from Him we can do nothing. As we dwell with Him and in Him, however, we become fruitful branches.

The next time we're about to rely on our own wisdom, let's choose instead to lay our anxiety and overwhelm at God's feet. Let's ask Him to help us go beneath the surface of our lives and heal the deeper longings and needs within us. Personally, there have been many times when I've set aside a day to fast, pray, and ask God to help me, heal me, and direct me in a certain area. Some of those times have been painful and humbling, but getting to the root of an issue with God's help is always refreshing and renewing. The Great Gardener can be trusted. He beckons us to find our strength and peace in Him.

The story is told of a little boy who was asked, "What is peace?" He answered, "Peace is when you feel all smooth inside."[9] As moms, we have numerous responsibilities tugging at us. Unexpected challenges are thrown at us daily. But even though life may not bring tranquillity on the outside, we can still feel smooth and calm on the inside. Overwhelm can be transformed into personal peace when we place our hearts, our lives—and yes, our calendars—in the Gardener's care.

Calming Thoughts

Scripture Reading: Psalm 40, "Finding Joy in Him"

Quiet Meditations:

- On whom does the psalmist rely? On whom do you rely?
- Underline the word *joy* (or *happy* or *rejoice*, depending on your Bible translation).
- What do you notice about the joyful person in this psalm?

Personal Prayer:

I praise You, Lord! You are my rock, my strength, and my redeemer. I confess that I often rely on myself instead of relying on You for my strength. Help me to look to You first. Thank You for always being with me, for always giving me help and hope. Guide me and give me wisdom in how to use my time. Show me clearly what I am supposed to do, and keep me from doing things simply to follow the crowd. May everything I do bring honor to You and blessing to others. In Jesus' name, amen.

step
one

Create a Calm Environment

All men desire peace, but very few desire those things that make for peace.

THOMAS À KEMPIS

By wisdom a house is built,
and through understanding it is established;
through knowledge its rooms are filled
with rare and beautiful treasures.

PROVERBS 24:3–4 NIV

A calm environment doesn't just happen. We must be intentional about creating a peaceful atmosphere, and as we do, we begin to effectively lessen the level of stress in our home.

3

Solutions to the Top Ten Stressors at Home

You cannot solve a problem until you acknowledge that you have one and accept responsibility for solving it.

ZIG ZIGLAR

Good sense will protect you;
understanding will guard you.

PROVERBS 2:11

What sends you? By that I mean, what really rattles you or stresses you out to the point of losing your temper or your sanity? The answer is probably a little different for each of us. For some, it's a messy or cluttered house. For others, it's having too many kids in the house at one time. For still others, it's trying to get out the door to make it to a parent-teacher meeting on time.

The fact is, if we are going to create a calm environment in our homes, we need to identify the stress points that tend to drive us over the edge and look at ways to reduce their impact upon us. To help us do that, I want to propose a Big Ten list of stressors that tend to rattle moms the most. As we consider each item on the list, keep three things in mind. First, our goal is not to do away with stress completely. Rather, it's to manage stress and work around it in a healthy and positive way, so that we don't emotionally annihilate every person living in our homes.

Second, you may not personally deal with all of the stressors in the Big Ten list. Maybe only three or four of them really send you into a tailspin. We all have different boiling points on different issues. What stresses me out may not bother you, and vice versa. Go ahead and zero in on the stress points that affect you, and simply skim the others.

Third, none of the items on the list are necessarily bad in and of themselves. But good, bad, or otherwise, if they cause considerable stress in our lives, then they must be addressed. See if you can identify with any of the following mom-rattling stressors:

The Big Ten Mom Stressors

1. House Beautiful: wanting the house to always look clean and nice
2. Perfect Kids: wanting to maintain a stellar family image
3. Need Nabbers: feeling needed by everyone at the same time
4. Guilt Grabbers: not meeting up to your own or others' expectations
5. Calendar Chaos: having too many activities and too many places family members need to be
6. Brain Swirl: having too many things to remember and do
7. Time Crunchers: feeling boxed in by deadlines, events, and obligations
8. Financial Struggles: trying to make ends meet, pay off debt, or pay bills
9. Daily Routines: dealing day in and day out with the before-school rush, after-school homework, and dinner and bedtime routines

10. The Unexpected: broken arms, forgotten homework, drop-in guests, and calls from school

Did you see your life in any of the stressors listed above? Take a moment to underline the ones that seem to affect you most. If you end up underlining every single one of them, don't let that bother you! If you have living, breathing human beings dwelling under your roof, then you're going to have a certain amount of stress in your life. It comes with the territory. Your task is to learn how to manage it by minimizing the avoidable stressors and dealing with the remaining stress in a positive manner.

Practical Defrazzlement

If you're like me, you want realistic and doable solutions to your problems. As we take a look at each of the Big Ten Mom Stressors, I'm going to suggest practical ways that you can change directions from feeling frazzled to experiencing more calm. It's up to you to glean from these suggestions what works best for you, based on your unique personality and family situation.

Following my suggestions for dealing with each stressor, I include a "Getting to the Roots" section designed to help you take your problem-solving plans to a deeper level and weed out the underlying issues that cause or add to your stress. Yes, we want to take care of surface stress, but we also need to get to the roots! Otherwise, just like a weed, our stress will eventually return. I also include a section called "Scripture Solution" to give you biblical support for making the changes that are necessary in your life.

Before we begin our practical defrazzlement, I want to share a paragraph with you that was first printed in *Christian Digest*. The author is unknown. It sets the stage for our pursuit of more calm and less stress:

There are two things, at least, about which we should never worry. First, the things we can't help. If we can't help them, worrying is certainly most foolish and useless. Secondly, the things we can help. If we can help them, let us set about it, and not weaken our powers by worry. Weed your garden. Pluck up the smallest roots of worry. Watch for their first appearance above the ground and pluck them while they are small. Don't let them get a start. They will crowd out all the beautiful things that ought to grow in our hearts unless we do.[1]

Great motivation, don't you think? Now let's "set about" finding our solutions to the Big Ten.

House Beautiful

Active kids and neatly kept houses do not necessarily go together. It may be difficult for many of us, but it is imperative that we separate ourselves from the desire for housekeeping perfection. The good news is we can make positive compromises to create less stress on ourselves and our family members. Here are a few ideas:

- Create a realistic housecleaning plan.
- Set a minimum goal of what must be done in order to maintain your sanity.
- Set a maximum goal of what you would like your house to look like on certain occasions.
- Divide chores and errands among the kids in age-appropriate ways.
- Give clear instructions to family members.
- Provide proper places for toys and other items to "belong."

Getting to the Roots

If House Beautiful is a stress point for you, then you may struggle with one or more of these issues: placing your security in having everything in its place; needing to be in control; wanting others to think you are a great housekeeper or have a perfect house (i.e., pride); or trying to please the hubby (or in-law or neighbor) who makes you feel guilty if the house is not perfect. Are you willing to release your "perfect picture" and find your security and strength in the Lord, not your environment? Are you able to talk to your husband or kids (or yourself) and develop a compromise with realistic expectations?

Scripture Solution: Luke 10:41–42

In this well-known passage, Martha was upset that her sister, Mary, was listening to Jesus rather than helping her prepare the food. Jesus addressed her and said, "Martha, Martha, you are worried and upset about many things. Only one thing is important. Mary has chosen the better thing, and it will never be taken away from her." Of course, Jesus wasn't saying that we should drop all our household responsibilities and go to Bible studies all the time. But He was getting to the root of the House Beautiful mentality. We have to ask ourselves, what's really important?

Perfect Kids

Can you imagine living day in and day out with an older person continually demanding that we look, act, and perform perfectly? What an absurd expectation to have placed upon us as adults! Yet many of us are tempted to place that same burden of perfection on our children. Have we become a society that has forgotten that it's okay to fall down and get hurt? Often our scrapes and bruises teach us life lessons we could learn no other way. All of us—children and adults—tend to learn best through our struggles, shortcomings, mistakes, and failures. Here are just a few thoughts to help us lighten up:

- Make a list of character qualities you want your children to learn.
- Focus on character more than image or achievement.
- Work together with your kids to form realistic goals.
- Realize that "looking precious" is not as important as *being* precious.
- Consider disappointments as opportunities to learn and do better next time.

Getting to the Roots

If you wrestle with wanting your kids to maintain an image of perfection, the deeper struggle may be pride, expectations that are too high, comparisons with others, issues from your own past, caring too much about what people think, or living vicariously through your children. Will you give the expectations you have for your children to the Lord and ask Him to direct their paths and yours? Are you willing to take that picture of perfection off the wall and lay it at Jesus' feet, recognizing that kids aren't perfect, spouses aren't perfect, and moms aren't perfect?

Scripture Solution: Matthew 6:33

In the Sermon on the Mount, Jesus addressed the issue of worry and overconcern about matters that aren't as important as we think (such as having perfect children). "The thing you should want most," He said, "is God's kingdom and doing what God wants. Then all these other things you need will be given to you." I want to want what's really important, don't you?

Need Nabbers

Don't you wish you had just a few more hands? Maybe several clones would be nice! Why is it that when one child needs you, all the children need you—usually at the time when you were just about to sit down and have five minutes to yourself? You love your kids; you just don't enjoy the constant tug on your energy. It's enough to send you sometimes! Here are a few suggestions to help you:

- Acknowledge your child's need by looking him or her in the eye and speaking kindly.

- Determine if it is an immediate need or one that can wait.

- Delegate what you can. Teach older kids to do their own laundry, pack their own lunches, etc.

- Encourage your children to use patience in waiting for your help.

- Remember that it's not healthy for your kids to have you at their every beck and call.

- If you have many kids with many needs, seek out appropriate help.

- Realize that this stage in your family life will pass. Ask the Lord for strength for the moment and for the day.

- Recheck your list of responsibilities to see if anything on it is unnecessary or can wait.

Getting to the Roots

If you feel like you want to scream at your family's constant barrage of needs, understand that your emotions may be influenced by your time of life, the time of the month, and/or the number of kids you have. Deeper issues may include the "supermom" syndrome (feeling as though you must be the one to solve everyone's problems), the inability or unwillingness to delegate, and impatience (theirs and/or yours). Will you allow others in your family to take on more responsibility? Are you willing to ask God for His patience, strength, wisdom, and help?

Scripture Solution: Romans 12:12

Paul gives the early Christians this encouragement in Romans 12:12: "Be joyful because you have hope. Be patient when trouble comes, and pray at all times." When we feel pulled in all directions, we can apply these words to our own situations, looking to God for hope and help.

Guilt Grabbers

Who among us doesn't know the unpleasant nudge of guilt? We have guilt because we didn't pick up the laundry; guilt because we couldn't attend our kid's soccer game; guilt because we never seem to be able to do enough—and the list goes on. Argh! Those little claws of guilt love to grab us and agitate us. Here are some ways to combat the guilt grabbers:

- Determine the source of your guilt. Is it self-imposed, or does it come from someone else?
- Determine if your guilt is false guilt or the Holy Spirit actually nudging you.
- Discuss your thoughts with the person who seems to make you feel guilty.
- Recognize the assumptions you're making about what others are thinking.
- Ask forgiveness if necessary.
- Remember that God doesn't intend for you to be loaded down with guilt. He sent Jesus to pay the price for your sins. Rejoice in the fact that as a believer in Christ, you are forgiven!

Getting to the Roots

When guilt tries to grab you and entangle you, consider the possibility that you may be a certified people pleaser who doesn't want to let anyone down. Or you may be a perfectionist who can't seem to allow for the possibility of error. Guilt may also be a result of un-confessed sin, unforgiveness, or lack of self-control. Are you willing to release the need to please others or be perfect, recognizing that ultimately you serve God, not man? Will you ask God to reveal any other underlying issues that need to be dealt with or confessed?

Scripture Solution: Psalm 103:11–14

"As high as the sky is above the earth, so great is his love for those who respect him. He has taken our sins away from us as far as the east is from west. The LORD has mercy on those who respect him, as a father has mercy on his children. He knows how we were made; he remembers that we are dust." I'm so thankful that God doesn't hold on to our mistakes and sins! Isn't it wonderful to know that He doesn't intend for us to carry our own load of guilt?

Calendar Chaos, Brain Swirl, and Time Crunchers

These three mom stressors fit in the same suitcase. Don't you just wish you could take that suitcase and throw it overboard, while you relax on the deck of a smooth-sailing cruise ship? Now back to reality! We may not be able to throw away all the responsibilities and activities that we juggle on a daily basis, but we can learn ways to successfully get a handle on them. Since many of the practical solutions I'm about to suggest fit all three stress points, I've put them together for your convenience. Hopefully they'll help you navigate the fast lane with a little more ease:

- Remember what we learned in chapter 2. Don't do everything; do the right things.
- Keep one main monthly calendar on which all family-member activities are entered.
- Write down your responsibilities for the week on sticky

notes. Place them on the refrigerator, a memo board, or some other place where you will see them each day. Pull them off as you accomplish each task or responsibility.

● Make Sunday a day of worship and rest. Take some time to regroup and pray through the coming week.

● Create a daily to-do list. Rate the items on the list as A ("must be done"), B ("would love to get done"), or C ("will get done if there's any time left after A and B"). Write your to-do list the night before, so you know what time you need to get up and get going the next day.

● Use file folders to keep and manage fliers, bulletins, and invitations. Consider having twelve file folders (one for each month) or one file folder per family member.

● Take a candid look at the responsibilities and activities involving you and your family members. Write them all down on a legal pad. Ask God to direct you and help you decide which ones are necessary and which ones should be dropped, changed, or postponed.

● Wisely step out of unnecessary activities, but don't drop the ball on responsibilities. If at all possible, carry them out until they're done.

● Remind yourself that August/September (start of school), December (Christmas), and May/June (end of school) will be slightly busier and more stressful than other months. Persevere, knowing that things will smooth out.

● Check out personal organizing systems. You may prefer an electronic, hand-held PDA. I still prefer the old-fashioned notebook-style calendar. (My favorite comes from the FranklinCovey Store in Dallas. You can go on-line at FranklinCovey.com to quickly find an organizer that works best for you.)

- Only agree to do jobs or take on responsibilities outside the home that employ your strengths, gifts, and
  talents. You'll be drained quickly if you get involved in
  something that plays to your weaknesses instead of
  your strengths.

Getting to the Roots

If you find that you are stressed out and overwhelmed because
too much is going on inside and outside your home, you may need
to examine issues such as people pleasing ("How can I say no?");
comparison ("Their family does it all, so why can't we?"); pride ("I
can do it all"); selfishness ("I want it all"); and fear ("If we don't do
it, my kids will fall behind"). You may have even deeper issues for
staying overly busy: covering up emotional hurt or pain, getting
away from a difficult spouse or family situation, or trying to make
up for your kids what you didn't do in your own childhood.

Are you willing to give your schedule over to God and ask for
wisdom, courage, and strength to say no when necessary? Will you
examine your motives for doing what you do? Will you submit to
God's leadership and direction in your life rather than simply follow
your own desires?

Scripture Solution: Proverbs 3:5–7

Solomon reminds us in this passage in Proverbs to seek God's direction: "Trust the LORD with all your heart, and don't depend on your own
understanding. Remember the LORD in all you do, and he will give you
success. Don't depend on your own wisdom. Respect the LORD and
refuse to do wrong." Wisdom brings life to those who pursue it!

Financial Struggles

Financial difficulties often affect our relationships, our personalities,
and the atmosphere in our homes. They definitely make our lives

more stressful. There are numerous reasons why we may find our-selves stretched financially, and finding solutions may take a lot longer than we would like; but we can begin today to progressively work toward family financial strength. Here are a few tips:

- Create a family budget to determine where your money is going and where you need to make adjustments.

- Go on a spending diet. Only buy necessities for a period of time. Use what you learn to change your spending habits.

- Seek out a wise financial planner or adviser to help you sort out your financial situation and develop a positive financial strategy.

- Begin to progressively work down your debt. If you are paying high interest rates for credit-card debt, consolidate your debt into a low-interest loan.

- Guard against credit-card spending. If you have trouble in this area, consider cutting up the cards.

- If you do use credit-cards, start the habit of paying them off every month.

Getting to the Roots

Financial struggles can be totally unexpected and circumstantial. Maybe your spouse has been laid off, or a family member has become seriously ill. Maybe your roof needs replacing ten years before you thought it would. But sometimes financial problems are self-imposed—the result of overspending and poor choices. If that's the case, you may want to examine possible underlying reasons, such as pride, the desire to "keep up with the Joneses," or the need to find security in material possessions. Some people even go on buying binges as a means of comfort (like eating chocolate). Are you willing to give your spending habits over to God? Will you ask for His direction in spending your money wisely?

Scripture Solution: 1 Corinthians 10:13

"The only temptation that has come to you is that which everyone has. But you can trust God, who will not permit you to be tempted more than you can stand. But when you are tempted, he will also give you a way to escape so that you will be able to stand it." For many of us, the temptation is to overspend; for others, it's to fret and worry about finances. Let's be responsible, seek help and advice when needed, and resist both kinds of temptation.

Daily Routines

"Grab your lunch, and don't forget the papers on the kitchen table!" And out the door you go, dashing to pick up the other kids in the carpool and get to school on time. Phew! What a morning! Then the rush starts again a few hours later when it's time to pick up the kids, get them to and from dance class and soccer practice, fix dinner, help with the homework . . . does it ever end?

Maybe your daily routine doesn't involve school-age kids. Maybe you have a baby that needs to be fed, changed, bathed, diapered, then fed again. The routines of life at any stage can tend to rattle us! Yet we rarely stop long enough in the middle of our routines to consider how things might be done better. Let's look at a few ideas:

- Take a step back and look at your routine. Which part (or parts) seems to stress you the most? What changes can be made to reduce stress in that area?
- Ask for help and/or hire it!
- Use easy dinner recipes and your Crockpot.
- Do as much as you can the night before. (Prepare lunches, make clothing decisions, gather homework, etc.)

- Find joy in the daily routine by turning your eyes upward and praying for your family and their friends. (I pray for my daughter's friends as I make her lunch each day. This changes my focus and gives me joy as I do something positive.)

- Ask a friend how you could do things differently. She may have a creative method, a fresh idea, or an easy recipe you never thought about.

- Maintain a heart and mind-set of thankfulness for the people in your life—and for their routines.

Getting to the Roots

Why does your daily routine send you sometimes? What's really going on inside? Perhaps you are dealing with one of these: guilt, knowing that you didn't prepare ahead of time; disorganization, causing you to always run late; pride, manifesting in a desire for everything to be perfect or in an obsession with being early or on time; or comparison, leading you to be frustrated with your own lack of creativity. Are you willing to accept responsibility for your routine and let go of things that really don't matter? Will you seek God's creativity for the best way to manage the daily things of life? Will you search for His joy in the midst of your routine?

Scripture Solution: 1 Thessalonians 5:16–18

The Apostle Paul closed his letter to the Thessalonians with a positive admonishment: "Always be joyful. Pray continually, and give thanks whatever happens. That is what God wants for you in Christ Jesus." We need to look for reasons to be joyful in the midst of our daily routines. We need to pray and keep on praying. And we need to continually give thanks; that's the natural thing for a joyful person to do.

The Unexpected

It happens just when you think you can't take on another responsibility or handle one more thing. *Brrrring!* The phone rings, and the school nurse tells you that your daughter broke her arm on the playground. The next few hours, days, and weeks are completely changed—filled now with doctor appointments, physical therapy sessions, and other necessary activities you never anticipated. This was definitely not on your well-planned schedule of to-dos! So how do you handle these "unexpected blessings"? Here are some thoughts:

- The moment you are informed of a change in plans (whether big or small), take a deep breath and pray, asking for God's help and strength to be flexible.

- Instead of choosing to be flustered, recognize that change is a normal part of life.

- Calmly call for help or backup.

- Recognize that you may need to step out of your normal routine, and that's okay. All family members need to adjust sometimes.

- Realize that you don't need to cook every meal or keep a perfectly clean house during this interval.

- Shift some of your responsibilities if necessary. Ask other people to take over for you. Generally, they will understand.

- Remain gracious and kind toward everyone involved. It may not be easy, but it will be a blessing in the long run—for you and for them. Plus you won't waste a lot of energy later on regret.

- Maintain a spirit of hope. Remember, God is with you. He will help you. Stay focused on the good things that are happening in the midst of the situation.

Getting to the Roots

If you tend to come unraveled when the unexpected takes place, you may have underlying issues such as fear, guilt, perfectionism, a need to find security in order, a need to be in control, or an inability to show grace toward others. Are you willing to relinquish control and fall into the hands of our loving Heavenly Father? Will you give your need for security, control, or perfection over to Him and allow Him to lead you safely through the unexpected?

Scripture Solution: Psalm 18:1–3

In many of the psalms, David reveals his complete trust in the Lord. I especially like this passage in Psalm 18: "I love you, LORD. You are my strength. The LORD is my rock, my protection, my Savior. My God is my rock. I can run to him for safety. He is my shield and my saving strength, my defender. I will call to the LORD, who is worthy of praise, and I will be saved from my enemies." When the unexpected happens, we need to make this our prayer as well.

That's Life

A wise person once said, "About the time you learn to make the most out of life, most of it is gone."[2] Sometimes the best solution for handling the stressors in life is to realize that in the big scheme of things, some of the little things that we get so stressed about are just that: little things. They really aren't that important. Dr. Richard Carlson created a best-selling book series on that premise. (*Don't Sweat the Small Stuff, Don't Sweat the Small Stuff for Teens, Don't Sweat the Small Stuff in Love, Don't Sweat the Small Stuff at Work* . . . and the list goes on and on.)

As Christians we really should be the poster children for anti-worry campaigns. Too often, however, we're just as stressed, worried, and rattled as everyone else. Jesus told His followers in the Sermon on the Mount that we are not to worry about the cares and concerns of this world; if our Heavenly Father takes care of the birds of the air and the lilies of the field, He will take care of you and me. Our focus should be on the blessings of the heavenly kingdom, not the cares and worries of this one.[3]

Oh, how easy it is to ignore Christ's charge to us! Perhaps the following poem will make you chuckle, as it did me. But its message is convicting:

> Said the robin to the sparrow,
> "I really do not know
> Why it is these human beings
> Rush about and worry so."
> Said the sparrow to the robin,
> "I think that it must be
> That they have no Heavenly Father,
> Such as cares for you and me."[4]

May our lives as women and as moms reflect the fact that we do have a Heavenly Father who cares for us! When the stressors of life come—whether they're in the Big Ten or the top one hundred—let's make sure our response is different from the world's. As God's children, let's determine to place our worries, cares, and challenges in our loving Father's hands.

Calming Thoughts

Scripture Reading: Matthew 6:25–33, "The Antiworry Sermon"

Quiet Meditations:
- In what ways does the Lord take care of you?
- Are there some areas of your life that you need to give over to God's care?
- What does it mean to you personally to "seek first God's kingdom"?

Personal Prayer:

Wonderful, loving Heavenly Father, I praise You for the mercy and care You have showered on me and my family. You are so good to us! Forgive me for all the times I've tried to solve the cares and problems in my life on my own. Help me to give them over to You instead. Help me, in the midst of my stress, to look to You. Give me the patience and self-control to stay calm. Lead me in Your wisdom to pull out the roots of those issues that cause me to feel rattled. Give me the strength I need to make the necessary changes in my life, so that in Your power I can have victory over stress. Thank You, Lord, for being with me always. In Jesus' name I pray, amen.

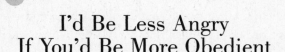

I'd Be Less Angry
If You'd Be More Obedient

Children need love, especially when they don't deserve it.

HAROLD HULBERT

When you are angry, do not sin, and be sure to stop being angry before the end of the day.

EPHESIANS 4:26

The person who said, "The more you grow up, the less you blow up," never met a stressed-out mom. Certainly, before we had children, we always thought we would be mature and self-controlled. We would never yell at our kids, as we had seen other mothers do. Then we had kids of our own, and our utopian theories flew out the window. Of course, if our kids would just be perfect little angels, then we wouldn't get so angry, right?

The true challenge for us as moms is to create a calm environment for our families, whatever the circumstances in our homes. If we wait for perfectly placid scenarios, we will be waiting a long time. Granted, it is easier to keep our cool when the kids are being obedient; but our calm shouldn't depend on their obedience. Our anger should be controlled by us, not them. How do we make that happen? That's what we're going to talk about in this chapter.

But hold on! Let's not let the kids off the hook too easily. Part of creating a calm environment *does* include teaching our children to value obedience, integrity, and respect. It has been said that "rearing children is like drafting a blueprint—you have to know where to draw the lines."[1] In this chapter we will also look at a positive plan for disciplining our children. *Wow,* you may be thinking, *does that mean that by the end of this chapter, not only will I have my anger under control, but my kids will be kind and obedient?* Well, I can't promise perfection. But I can help you get things moving in the right direction.

Taming the Angry Monster Inside

Ask a group of mothers to name their biggest area of personal struggle at home, and most of them would say "anger" or "screaming at the kids." Putting a finger on the moment each of us went from wonder woman to witch is difficult; but more than likely, it happened sometime around the first "no" that came out of our first child's mouth. Getting a grip on anger is a part of every mom's life. Some of us have higher tolerance levels than others, but we all have our boiling points.

So what can we do when we feel the heat rising, and we know we're about to let the kids have it? We can practice the STOP method:

S stands for "Step away from the situation." If you are at home, step into another room and away from the immediate source of tension. If you are at the grocery store, don't leave your kids alone; instead, take a few steps away from the shopping cart and remove yourself (at least to some degree) from the source of your anger.

T stands for "Take several deep, calming breaths." As you fill your lungs with fresh air, your body physically relaxes in the process. And by taking several breaths, you give yourself a little time to physically calm down and get ahold of yourself.

O stands for "Objectively look at the situation and employ self-control." You may discover there's more going on than first meets the eye. Perhaps the reason your son is throwing a temper tantrum is because he missed his nap, and he's understandably exhausted. Maybe your teenager had a rough day at school and is taking it out on everyone at home. Maybe you're experiencing PMS, and *you're* taking it out on everyone at home! Whatever the issue, make an effort to think objectively; don't simply explode due to surface tension.

P stands for "Pray." Silently or aloud, send up an immediate prayer to God and ask for His help, recognizing that you don't have what it takes to tame the anger monster on your own. A quick "Dear Lord, please help me to show self-control and not yell at my kids right now" brings the situation before God, allows you to draw on His infinite resources, and reminds you that you are not alone.

Of course, the STOP method is a short-term solution. It's helpful in those times of immediate need, when we're about to burst forth with rage and anger. But ultimately we need to get to the core issues behind our anger; otherwise we'll be STOPPING so much, our heads will spin. Why do we allow anger to take over and end up screaming at the ones we love? Here are some possible reasons:

- We don't realize how damaging our anger and screaming are to our kids.
- We're doing exactly what our mothers did.
- We have a deep-rooted bitterness (against a parent, a husband, or someone else), and it surfaces in anger.
- It's "that time of the month," and our hormones are pinging off the walls.
- We have grown comfortable with anger, and now it just seems to come naturally.
- We are physically weary, and we can't muster the self-control to stop ourselves.

- We have an area of sin in our lives that we haven't confessed or released to the Lord.
- We simply don't have the will power to resist screaming.

Please take a few minutes to prayerfully ask God to show you the root of your anger. It may be one of the items listed above, or it may be something beyond this list. Whatever the case, I want to encourage you to take it before the Lord, confess it, and ask for His help in overcoming your tendency toward anger. Then take positive steps to change your behavior. For example:

- Find an accountability partner who will ask you each week about how you're handling your anger.
- Keep a journal, writing out your thoughts and feelings. Release to the Lord any deep-seated areas of bitterness or resentment you may be harboring.
- Confess sin and turn from it.
- Remember that your kids learn best by your example. Your self-control will eventually beget self-control in your children. Anger, on the other hand, will eventually beget anger. Prayerfully break the cycle if you grew up in an angry household.
- Ask God every morning for His strength to ignore the urge to scream.
- Replace your scream with a whisper. It takes about as much energy to whisper as it does to scream, so lower your voice and whisper what you want to say to your children. They will have to be quiet to hear what you're saying. (Don't overuse this technique, however; they may grow callous to it.)

- Visit a biblically-based counselor if you sense that you need help in dealing with an abnormal amount of anger.

Keep in mind that a certain amount of anger is normal; the issue is, what do we do with that anger? The apostle Paul gives us good advice in his letter to the Ephesians:

> When you are angry, do not sin, and be sure to stop being angry before the end of the day. Do not give the devil a way to defeat you . . . When you talk, do not say harmful things, but say what people need—words that will help others become stronger. Then what you say will do good to those who listen to you. And do not make the Holy Spirit sad. The Spirit is God's proof that you belong to him. God gave you the Spirit to show that God will make you free when the final day comes. Do not be bitter or angry or mad. Never shout angrily or say things to hurt others. Never do anything evil. Be kind and loving to each other, and forgive each other just as God forgave you in Christ.[2]

Good advice for mothers, don't you think? We need to recognize the power our words have to set the tone for our homes. Angry words can set a negative tone; kind words can set a positive, peaceful tone. Solomon said, "A person's words can be life-giving water; words of true wisdom are as refreshing as a bubbling brook."[3] He added, "The tongue can kill or nourish life."[4]

We have a choice in how we use our tongues. Will we use them to refresh and nourish our children, setting a tone of peace, learning, and love? Or will we use our tongues to kill and destroy their spirits? Let's be builders, not demolishers! Yes, we will have times when we need to train and discipline our kids, but we can do these things in a calm and loving manner. It's much easier for our children to learn from calm, careful, and wise words of discipline than from out-of-control screams, cries, and shouts.

Careful and Wise Discipline

Of course it would take more than this chapter to fully cover the topic of discipline. Realistically we can only touch on a few key points here. Later you may want to read one or more books on the subject. Here are four of my favorites: *Shepherding a Child's Heart* by Tedd Tripp; *Faith Training* by Joe White; *Grace Based Parenting* by Tim Kimmel; and *Answering the Eight Cries of a Spirited Child* by Dave and Claudia Arp. You can find many other great books on discipline at your local Christian bookstore.

We often equate discipline with punishment, but the definition of the word is actually much broader. Discipline encompasses the idea of firm, measured, and gracious training. Sometimes that training involves punishment, and sometimes it doesn't.

As we discipline our children, we need to keep our eyes focused on the objective. In my house, that objective is to stamp out the three Ds: dishonesty, disrespect, and disobedience. I believe these are the three biggies that really matter in the long run in the character development of our children. It's so easy to get caught up in the minutiae of "clean your room," "eat your vegetables," and "do your homework" that we forget the greater goal of developing good character. Not that clean rooms, proper nutrition, and good study habits aren't important; but our training efforts need to be anchored in the things that matter most.

So what is the best way to discipline (or train) our precious charges and help them avoid the three Ds? The first step is to make sure we clearly teach and instruct them in what is right. That is, we need to teach them the opposite of the three Ds: honesty, respect, and obedience. How? One way is to use planned devotionals and lessons. Lessons from the Bible, in particular, give our children the firm foundation they need. We can teach honesty by going to such passages as Exodus 20:16; Proverbs 17:4, 20; or Ephesians 4:18–21. To teach respect, we can go to Romans 13, Colossians 3:8–25, or stories such as "The Good Samaritan" (Luke 10:25–37) or "The Woman at the Well" (John 4:1–42). To teach obedience, we can go to Ephesians 6:1–3; Exodus 20:12; or Colossians 3:20.

Another powerful way we can teach important life principles is by keeping our eyes open and taking advantage of "teachable moments" that arise along life's way. For instance, when you take your kids to the park, you can teach them to be thankful for God's creation and to respect it. When you're watching the news together, you can talk about the practical consequences of sin. When a friend at school betrays them, you can teach them through the pain about the value of being trustworthy.

Perhaps the most effective means for teaching life principles, however, is by our own example. If we want honest kids, then we must be honest, even in the little things. If we want respectful kids, then our kids need to see us showing respect toward other people—whether that's in the way we treat the waitstaff at a restaurant or the way we talk about the leaders of our country. If we want obedient kids, then they need to see that we value obedience by making sure we don't complain about laws or go against the rules. (Think speed limits on the roadways.) Remember, our kids learn best by watching us!

As we teach our children the right way to conduct themselves, we also need to be clear about the consequences of wrong behavior. Our kids need to know that if they choose to be dishonest, disrespectful, or disobedient, they will face swift and certain consequences to help them learn to not do it again. In other words, when our kids do something wrong (and they will), we must move toward the punishment phase of discipline.

Punishment must be handled wisely, with learning as the goal. We need to ask ourselves, "What am I trying to teach here? What's the best way for my children to learn from this?" We should never punish our children in anger; rather, we should wait until we have gained our composure to administer consequences. We must make sure our kids understand why they are being punished and what is expected of them in the future.

Figuring out the right punishment can be a daunting task. The truth is, in order for punishment to be an effective training tool, it must be painful. If you send your daughter to her room as punishment for talking back to you, yet she enjoys going to her room to play with her dolls, then you really haven't punished her. If, on the other hand, you take away her television privileges and she has to miss her favorite shows, then you have made it hurt. She'll think twice before talking disrespectfully again.

Sometimes we can simply use the natural consequences of our children's behavior to make our point. Let's say you ask the kids not to toss the ball in the house, yet one day they toss the ball in the family room and break a vase. The natural consequences may be that they have to clean up the mess and then do chores around the house to earn money to pay for a replacement. Of course, the chores must be hard work in order to make the strong impression: obedience matters!

As we discipline our kids, it's important that we don't simply react to surface behavior. Let's say your teenage daughter runs into the house crying, slamming the front door so hard that the glass in the door breaks. To simply punish her for breaking the glass would deal with the surface symptoms, but you'd be ignoring the pain that caused her to act the way she did.

Sometimes good discipline and training require that we ask questions, so we can find out what is really going on underneath our children's actions. We can learn a lot about our kids in the process. If your son gets in trouble at school, for example, the question, "What made you want to cheat on the test?" takes you beyond the wrong behavior to a deeper understanding of the pressures he may be struggling with and the root cause or sin. You still have to administer punishment, but you can also help him deal with the underlying issues so he'll never be tempted to cheat again.

Coming Together

A calm attitude and wise, careful discipline go together. Anger may lead to temporarily changed behavior, but it is not effective in long-term teaching and training. Screaming is effective in teaching one thing: how to scream. Since we don't want to raise young screamers, we should curb our own screams! As we've already said, our best teaching tool is our own example. If we want our kids to be honest, respectful, and obedient, we must begin by being honest, respectful, and obedient. Then, when we come to the place where we are able to discipline in a kind and loving way, with training as our goal, we'll introduce a new atmosphere in our homes: one that is characterized by more calm and less stress.

Calming Thoughts

Scripture Reading: Proverbs 15, "Gentle Words and Joyful Learning"

Quiet Meditations:
- Read through Proverbs 15 and underline all of the passages that speak about the virtue of reining in our anger and guarding our mouths. Read it through a second time, noting all the verses that teach about the importance of discipline.
- What is the Lord teaching you personally through these verses?
- What changes do you want to make in your own behavior and in the way you discipline your kids?

Personal Prayer:
Wonderful Heavenly Father, I praise You for being the Perfect Parent. Thank You for Your grace, Your mercy, and Your discipline. Thank You for Your Word and for Your Holy Spirit; they lead me and guide me through life. O Lord, I confess I have sometimes disciplined my children in anger. I have not looked to You for help in guarding my heart and my tongue. Help me to be patient and kind to everyone in my family, and give me the self-control I need to carefully discipline and wisely train my kids. Help me to be the example they need to see, so they will in turn live to honor You. In Jesus' name I pray, amen.

5

Winning the War on Piles of Stuff

*Cleaning your house while your kids are still growing
is like shoveling your walk before it stops snowing.*

PHYLLIS DILLER

*Wisdom will make your life pleasant
and will bring you peace.*

PROVERBS 3:17

True confession: I have five books on my shelf about how to organize your life, home, or office. Not one of them has helped me overcome the piles of stuff that keep growing and reappearing at my house. You've seen the bumper sticker that reads, "Stuff happens." Well, stuff does happen. It happens to pile up in almost every room of my house! I want and need real solutions to help me eliminate them—or at least minimize them.

There are some people who are born organized. The rest of us struggle to put a finger on the permission slip that was supposed to be signed last week or find matching clean socks for the kids. I'm the type who naturally tends toward disorganization. Thankfully (since the books on my shelf have hardly been cracked), God has placed certain people in my life to teach me organizing principles along the way.

Pile annihilation is a positive step toward creating a calm environment in our homes. Like it or not, it's a fact: Clutter adds stress to our lives. When we can't find the things we need, we become frustrated. We feel overwhelmed when we have loads of laundry or heaps of papers growing around us. Simply put, piles agitate us—and we could all use a little less agitation. So let's conquer!

From Chaos to Clutter Free

Where are your piles? Take a mental walk through your home and note the places that seem to accumulate papers, shoes, laundry, and other assorted items. If you're like me, you probably accumulate items in funny places for no apparent reason. I don't quite understand it, but out of the blue, with no planning whatsoever, a pile of papers will suddenly grow on my kitchen counter. If only flowers in my garden would grow so easily!

What can we do to keep the piles from growing? We must begin by changing a few habits and patterns. Don't worry. I know it's hard to change. I understand that the routines of our lives fit comfortably, like a pair of old slippers. But I also know that old slippers can get pretty ratty-looking after a while. Sometimes we need to replace those old slippers with new and better-looking ones.

Have you ever heard of the FlyLady? If you haven't discovered her Web site yet, I encourage you to visit it at www.FlyLady.net. Her name is a bit odd, I know; but the FlyLady is a great resource for practical solutions for keeping our homes clean and free from clutter. Her three-part approach makes sense:

1. Establish small routines first, then work up to more.
2. Be consistent.
3. Take your time and enjoy the process.

She writes:

Your home did not get dirty in one day, and it will not get clean in a day either. You have been living in clutter and chaos for many years; you are not going to get your home clean in a day. I do not want you to crash and burn. This is why I teach you to take baby steps. If you try to do this all at once, you are going to be mad at me, because this will be like every other "get-organized" method you have tried. I want you to take your time. As you establish one habit, you will very easily be able to add another one to your routines.[1]

Let's apply some of the FlyLady's principles to our own homes room by room. Research tells us it takes approximately twenty-one days to form a new habit. I must be a slow learner, since it usually takes me a month to establish a new habit or routine! With new habits as our goal, then, let's commit the next four weeks to developing one new routine. By the end of that time, the routine should be so ingrained in us that it has become an integral part of our lifestyle. Then we can move on to add another routine the next month.

Don't panic! Honestly, if we got out a stopwatch and timed each of the routines we're about to consider, we would discover that each one by itself only takes a few minutes. De-cluttering really isn't a matter of time; it's a matter of habit. So let's get started!

The Kitchen

We'll begin in the most-used room in the house: the kitchen. Choose one of the following routines to begin this month. Remember, we're talking baby steps here—only add one routine at a time:

- Keep the sink clean. If you have a double sink, at least one side should be dish free. This may include emptying the dishwasher every day, so those dirty dishes have a place to go.

- Don't allow a mail pile to develop. Stand by the trash can as you open mail. Throw away junk mail; put bills to be paid in a file (that's *file*, not *pile*); distribute personal mail to different members of the house (perhaps in designated boxes in their bedrooms); and put things you need to read in the room where you're most likely to read them. Be guarded and realistic about what you set aside to read!

- Make sure all counters are cleaned and clear when you go to bed each night—no food, no dishes, no piles of mail, no papers from school. Wipe down the counters right before you go to bed. You'll be amazed at how much happier you'll be in the morning when you walk into a clean, clutter-free kitchen.

The Family Room

The next room to conquer is the family room. Here are three new habits you can start, one each month:

- Put toys back in their proper places each night. You may need to purchase a toy box, shelves, or a heavy plastic bin to give toys and children's books a place to belong. Make it a nightly routine, and enlist your kids (yes, even toddlers) to help in the process. Make it fun and simple. If you have older kids, get them to pick up their schoolwork and projects and prepare their backpacks before going to bed.

- Choose one day a week to reorganize the bins and shelves. It may be a lot of work the first time; but week by week, it will become less of a hassle. Pitch out or give away unused, broken, or unneeded items. Throw away newspapers and old magazines unless you can use them later for school projects. If you need to keep them, put them in a storage place out of sight.

- Choose another day during the week to dust. I like to keep a little packet of dust wipes hidden in the den. Then it takes just a few minutes to wipe over the surfaces. As I dust, I eliminate any piles that may have begun to accumulate, such as school papers, magazines, or TV guides.

The Bathroom

Now it's time to set things in order in the bathroom. Add only one of the following routines every four weeks:

- Always hang and fold; never drape or drop. Place towels and clothes in their correct spaces. Remember, it takes just a few seconds more to place something on a hanger or hook. Put dirty clothes directly into the dirty-clothes hamper.

- Clean your counters as you go. As you put on your makeup, put everything back in its proper place. It's just as easy to put it in the right place as to leave it out. When you are finished with a wet washcloth, use it to wipe off the counter, then put it in the hamper or hang it to dry. Or keep cleaning wipes in a dispenser in the cupboard; that makes a fresh wipe easy to grab.

- Clean out one drawer, cupboard, or portion of a closet per week. Take fifteen minutes to clean, reorganize, and throw out things that you don't need or can't use.

The Bedroom

Add one of these routines each month to keep your bedroom straight:

- Make your bed every morning. This is essential for making you feel that you have a clean house.

- Put dirty clothes in the clothes hamper. If you don't have one, buy one. There are many cute clothes hampers in stores these days! Buy one that will motivate you and your husband to place your dirty clothes in it. Put away clean laundry in closets and drawers; don't give it a temporary resting place (for example, on the top of your dresser or at the foot of your bed). It only takes a few extra seconds to put clean clothes in their proper places.

- Give books, papers, jewelry, and other collectables (things that tend to make piles) a proper home. Create designated spaces for them, and return them to those spaces whenever you are finished with them.

Did you notice that if we put all four rooms together, we have twelve routines, one for each month of the year? Each one is a simple, positive habit that can significantly reduce stress in our lives if we'll just get it ingrained into our systems. Your family members will also benefit as they participate with you. Try your best to stick with each habit; but use wisdom in allowing for a little flexibility, recognizing that there will be times when you just can't get it done.

Did you also notice that several of the routines encourage you to choose one day per week to implement the habit? You may find it helpful to spread these out over a week; for instance, designate fifteen minutes on Mondays to clean out a drawer, fifteen minutes on

Wednesdays to reorganize the toy bin, and fifteen minutes on Fridays to dust the family room.

Your routines may end up looking a little different from the twelve I've suggested here. Feel free to personalize your pile plan to meet the needs in your own home. And don't forget to pray about your piles. I know that sounds a little funny; but remember, God cares about the details of your life, and annihilating piles is one of those details. Ask God to give you creativity and discipline in forming good pile-killing habits. Yes, I believe in praying about everything!

To Be Read or to Do

Two of my biggest piles are the ones I tend to put off more than others: the pile of things I want to read, and the pile of things I need to respond to. I used to keep magazines, for example, if the headlines of one or two articles piqued my interest. I have begun to greatly reduce my "To Read" pile, however, by adding one simple routine: When I buy a magazine or get one in the mail, I quickly skim through it to see if there are any articles I really want to read. Then I tear or clip out those articles and place them in a file or other appropriate place where I know I will read them.

In my present lifestyle, there are two times when I deliberately read: on Sunday afternoons and in the evening just before bed. I save some of the articles to read on Sunday and some to read just before bed. If there is information in the article that I think I may need for reference later on, I place it in a file in my filing cabinet.

Then there's the "To Do" pile, which includes important letters I need to write, invitations I need to respond to, and projects I must do. I go through this pile on a regular basis to try to reduce it as much as possible. Once a week would be ideal; but I must admit, sometimes it's more like once a month. I need to get into a better routine!

What are your most demanding piles? Take a moment to consider practical solutions for eliminating or reducing them. Make a plan and tell it to someone who can give you feedback and perhaps hold you accountable. Then begin to take action.

My friends Amy and Leslie are my prayer partners as well as my accountability partners. We bounce ideas off each other all the time. We share everything from quick recipes to tips for cleaning out a garage. When one of us is stuck on a problem and not quite sure how to solve it, we talk about it and help find a solution together. If you have a pile or an area of your home that you don't seem to be able to conquer, try getting a friend's candid perspective. Most likely, she can offer advice, provide accountability, and maybe even help with those boxes in the garage.

Jennifer's Gems

Earlier in this chapter we said that some people are born organized. My friend Jennifer is one of them. She is the mother of two young girls and the founder of a business that helps people organize their homes and their lives.[2] I've asked her to give us some words of wisdom from her business and personal experience. She offers five key points for creating calm out of chaos:

1. Everything needs a home. When something enters your house, it must have a place to go; otherwise it simply gets lost in a sea of chaos on the countertops or in piles on the floor.

2. Learn to purge. Keep a box in the garage to collect anything from your house that you want to donate to charity or sell. If you want to be really ambitious, staple a clear baggie containing masking tape and a permanent marker to the box, and immediately price any items you hope to sell at a garage sale.

3. Allow your space to limit you. We are all blessed with a certain amount of space, and overfilling it is like dou-

bling the recipe without increasing the size of the pan! You're just making a mess for yourself to clean up. For example, if your closet is full of clothes already, either purge what you have to make room for more, or don't bring any more in!

4. Call for help. Delegate responsibilities as much as possible. Expecting your family members to share in running errands, cleaning, and meal preparation will help you, and it will create a spirit of teamwork in your home. If a busy schedule limits your abilities, don't hesitate to hire a cleaning service once a month or a professional organizer to come in and help get your home in order.

5. Align your perspective. Directing your eyes to the Lord and submitting your daily plans to Him is the most important aspect of organizing your life. It's taking your to-do list and lifting it up to the heavens, saying, "I am here only because of You, Lord, and my desire is that You be glorified by what I accomplish today. Please order my steps."

If She Can Do It, We Can Do It

I want to close this chapter by introducing you to one more incredibly organized woman. Marcie Hatfield is a pastor's wife and the mother of five kids. She is also the leader of the women's ministry in her church and, like Jennifer, a professional organizer. Given her numerous responsibilities, being organized is an absolute imperative! How does she do it with such limited time and a full schedule? I'll let Marcie tell you herself:

I grew up in a small home with a family of six where everyone shared a room. Now I am a mother of five and continue to think of space as a commodity. I am married to a wonderful pastor, so my family is quite busy. I also believe the

Bible is true, so one of my lifetime goals is to obey Romans 12:13 (NIV): "Practice hospitality!" Practice means to do over and over again!

In order to teach my children to be hospitable and for our family to live amidst all the clutter that bombards us daily, I have found the following tips help me not only to survive, but to win the war over piles of stuff:

- Break down your challenge into manageable pieces. Begin on a small section and watch how your motivation grows.
- Work when you are fresh. No distractions! (Barter with a friend to watch your kids, and do not answer the phone!)
- Have bins, containers, and boxes ready to sort your piles.
- Set up a hub for household papers. I have a file folder for each family member; important papers live there until they are needed.
- Eighty percent of what we file is never looked at again. Make good decisions about what you choose to file.
- Find a personal organizer that fits your personality (or put one together yourself). Make an appointment with yourself every night to review your calendar. Know exactly what your plan will be for the next day before you go to sleep at night.

Always remember, people are more important than things. Begin with yourself, changing and managing the piles in your home. Then you can feel free to practice hospitality toward those people you love . . . over and over again! You can do it![3]

Like Marcie, Jennifer, and the indomitable FlyLady, we have the ability to make our homes havens of calm and order. All we have to do is add a few simple routines to our lives one at a time. Not only will we reduce our levels of stress, but we will open up opportunities to show hospitality and love to the people around us. Believe it: The battle against clutter is a war worth winning!

Calming Thoughts

Scripture Reading: Psalm 51, "A Clean Heart in a Clean House"

Quiet Meditations:

- As you get your home in order, what areas of your heart need cleansing?
- What piles tend to accumulate in your life? Are there any piles of worry, envy, or bitterness you need to remove?
- To whom does the psalmist look to clean his heart?

Personal Prayer:

Glorious Father and Creator, I praise You for the incredible way You have created this universe. The order in Your creation is beautiful to observe! I praise You for being a holy God of order. I confess that I struggle with _____. [Fill in the blank; for example, you might say, "the self-discipline to keep things in order," or "an obsession with having everything in order."] O Lord, help me to find a healthy balance, so I can honor You in my home. Show me the best plan to de-clutter and overcome the piles. Help me to have victory in the small steps and simple routines. Thank You, Lord, that I am never alone and that You care about the details of my life. In Jesus' name I pray, amen.

step
two

Refresh Your Spirit

The miracle, or the power, that elevates the few is to be found in their industry, application, and perseverance under the prompting of a brave, determined spirit.

MARK TWAIN

The law of the LORD is perfect,
*   reviving the soul.*
The statutes of the LORD are trustworthy,
*   making wise the simple.*
The precepts of the LORD are right,
*   giving joy to the heart.*
The commands of the LORD are radiant,
*   giving light to the eyes.*

PSALM 19:7–8 NIV

Calm begins in our own spirits, as God gives us His peace. The world around us may be chaotic, but we can experience calm in our hearts through His strength and power.

6

Prescription for Peace

Peace does not dwell in outward things, but within the soul.
FRANÇOIS FÉNELON

Now may the Lord of peace give you peace at all times and in every way. The Lord be with all of you.
2 THESSALONIANS 3:16

Could you use a prescription for peace? Several months ago I asked a friend of mine, a mother of four, to compile a list of times when a typical mom could use a healthy dose of inner peace. She gave me her own personal list, which we agreed we could probably sell for a good sum of money to a writer for a comedy sitcom. Here's what she wrote:

You know you could use a prescription for peace when

1. A new neighbor calls to tell you she's heard wonderful things about your awesome family and what godly children you have. While she is talking, you are holding your hand over the mouthpiece, telling your son to quit hitting his brother.

2. You find evidence around the house that one of your two dogs is very sick. You confine one dog to the laundry room, only to find out a few hours later that the second dog is the sick one.

3. Your car is soaking wet on the inside, even though you asked the kids to roll up the windows the night before because the weatherman said, "Eighty percent chance of rain tomorrow."

4. Your husband forgot to pay the utility bill, and your water is turned off by the utility company two hours before your dinner guests arrive.

5. You switch dogs—let the first one out of confinement in the laundry room and put the second one in—only to find out in a few hours that the first dog has become ill too.

6. Your son tells you at 9:55 p.m. that he needs graph paper and a poster board tonight. You run to the store right before it closes. When you get home, your son tells you he now needs a new glue stick to replace the one the dog ate while confined in the laundry room.

7. You tell your son that even though he has his driving permit, you will back the car up, because he "needs to learn" by watching you. You back over the barbecue pit, which is filled with burning coals and catches the neighbors' grass on fire. (These are the same neighbors who have complained several times about what your dogs have done to their grass.)

8. Your daughter begs you for a certain shirt at the mall. You save up, run to the mall, and surprise your daughter with the shirt—at which point she tells you that she doesn't want it anymore, because someone else at school already has it.

9. Your kids say you're mean because you won't let them have another dog.

No doubt a prescription for peace is something every mom could use—including (quite obviously) my dear friend. Recently I came across a box of greeting cards at a gift shop. Each card was imprinted with the following quote: "Peace. It does not mean to be in a place where there is no noise, trouble, or hard work. It means to be in the midst of those things and still be calm in your heart."[1] That's a great definition of peace. The question is, how is it possible to have peace and calm within our hearts when we have trials and challenges all around us?

God writes us a prescription for peace in His Word. You may be surprised that it's not a simple antidote of "If I do this and this and this, then God will grant me peace." No, in God's prescription, peace comes through chewing on God's Truth and allowing a new perspective on peace to permeate our hearts and lives. The prescription is a process of discovery. In this chapter we'll begin that process and discover answers to questions such as these:

- Where does peace come from?
- How does peace develop in my life?
- Why don't I feel peaceful?
- If God wants me to have peace, then why do I have so much turmoil?

In his book *Finding Peace*, Charles Stanley writes, "The world regards peace as being the by-product of doing the right deeds, saying the right words, working in the right job, or having the right intentions. These aren't at all the criteria for peace described in God's Word. Peace is an inner quality that flows out of a right relationship with God."[2] In other words, peace is the result of a continuing, growing relationship with God. Peter put it this way: "Grace and peace be given to you more and more, because you truly know God and Jesus our Lord."[3] Our journeys toward peace unfold only as we get to know God and the truths of His Word.

Peace Comes from God, Not Circumstances

Jesus taught that it is possible to have peace in the midst of troubles. In fact, just when His own disciples were about to face their biggest challenge (Jesus' crucifixion), He offered them the gift of peace. He said, "I leave you peace; my peace I give you. I do not give it to you as the world does. So don't let your hearts be troubled or afraid."⁴ Later the same night He said, "I told you these things so that you can have peace in me. In this world you will have trouble, but be brave! I have defeated the world."⁵

Isn't it comforting to know that our wonderful God is the giver of peace? I don't know about you, but I can't generate a whole lot of peace on my own. Thankfully, peace is one of the fruit of God's Spirit in our lives. And that peace—God's peace—is different from the peace the world tries to offer. According to the world's definition, peace is something external. It has to do with circumstances. If there is no war, no struggle, no turmoil, then the world says, "peace." But the peace God offers is not external; it's internal and eternal.

The Bible mentions three kinds of peace: peace between God and man, peace between Christians, and peace within a person's heart. God provides peace in each of these areas. Jesus was the provision of peace between sinful man and Holy God. The Bible says, "Therefore, since we have been made right in God's sight by faith, we have peace with God because of what Jesus Christ our Lord has done for us."⁶ How wonderful to know that we are not the enemies of God! We are at peace with God through faith in Jesus.

The Holy Spirit joins us together in peace with other believers. Paul wrote to the Ephesians, "Always be humble, gentle, and patient, accepting each other in love. You are joined together with peace through the Spirit, so make every effort to continue together in this way."⁷ When it comes to peace with our brothers and sisters in Christ, we have an obligation to make an effort toward peace. God's Spirit unifies us with peace; therefore, it is fitting that we be humble, gentle, patient, and loving toward one another, creating an atmosphere of peace between us.

The third type of peace refers to a sense of refreshment in our spirits and a calm within our hearts. It is the inner peace that is talked about throughout the Scriptures. Isaiah referred to it as "true peace" or "perfect peace."[8] Paul referred to it as "God's peace, which is so great we cannot understand it."[9] The Bible is clear that the God of Peace is the One who gives us this kind of peace. It doesn't come from formulas. It doesn't come from our own efforts, or even from our strength of character. It comes from God. The essence of God's character is peace. I like the way Paul closes his letter to the Romans: "And now may God, who gives us his peace, be with you all."[10]

Peace through Prayer

How exactly does God give us His peace? How does the transfer take place from His heart to ours? Thankfully, God has given us an effective tool for experiencing His peace: the power of prayer. Perhaps you have wondered, why do we pray if God already knows our needs? We pray because God tells us to—and because He does a powerful work in our lives as we spend time with Him. He gives us peace through the process of prayer. Each of the four main elements of prayer—praise, confession, thanksgiving, and supplication (making requests)—brings us peace in a unique way.

Praising God certainly brings us peace. When we praise God, we recognize His powerful attributes. We remind ourselves that He is sovereign, powerful, and holy. Praise takes us out of a place of anxiety and worry and into a place of hope and trust and peace. That's what David discovered. Take some time to reflect on the Book of Psalms, and notice how David's praises to the Lord led him to experience both peace and joy. Praise will do the same for each of us. As David wrote in Psalm 34, "Examine and see how good the LORD is. Happy is the person who trusts him."[11]

Confession also brings us peace. As David brought his confessions before the Lord, his spirit was renewed. In Psalm 51 David offered this prayer of confession: "Turn your face from my sins and wipe out all my guilt. Create in me a pure heart, God, and make my spirit right again."[12] Of course, as Christians our sins are forgiven through Christ's death on the cross. Yet confession is still an important part of prayer; it's a recognition of Christ's sacrifice and an admission of our continued need for God's mercy and grace. There is great peace and spiritual renewal to be found in leaving our sorrow and guilt at the Lord's feet! "If we say we have no sin, we are fooling ourselves, and the truth is not in us," the apostle John wrote. "But if we confess our sins, he will forgive our sins . . . He will cleanse us from all the wrongs we have done."[13]

Thanking God is another aspect of prayer that brings us peace. When an attitude of gratitude fills our minds and hearts, our eyes are focused on God's blessings and all the good things He has done for us, rather than on our circumstances, worries, and fears. As Paul wrote to the Philippians, "Do not worry about anything, but pray and ask God for everything you need, always giving thanks. And God's peace, which is so great we cannot understand it, will keep your hearts and minds in Christ Jesus."[14]

Notice the connection Paul made between giving thanks and asking God for "everything you need." Giving our requests to the Lord is the fourth aspect of prayer that brings us peace. As we practice bringing every aspect of our lives—including our needs, worries, and desires—to God in prayer, He becomes our rock and our refuge. We come to a place of trust—not in ourselves or circumstances or other people, but in our sovereign and powerful God. Isaiah wrote, "You [God] will keep in perfect peace all who trust in you, whose thoughts are fixed on you! Trust in the LORD always, for the LORD GOD is the eternal Rock."[15]

I love the way the writer of Hebrews encouraged the early Christians to pray: "So let us come boldly to the throne of our gracious God. There we will receive his mercy, and we will find grace to help us when we need it."[16] Now that's a place of peace!

A Perspective, Not a Feeling

At this point you may be thinking, *I know that peace comes from God. I pray to Him faithfully. So why don't I feel peaceful?* Well, what do you think peace should feel like? A warm, fuzzy emotion? A totally relaxed body? A restful mental state of nirvana?

I think peace eludes many of us because we don't really know what we're looking for. What if I told you that peace is not some wonderful, euphoric feeling? Disappointed? If peace were simply a feeling, then it would come and go based on our moods, our health, and our circumstances. Now peace may *result* in a nice feeling. But peace is not a feeling; it's a perspective. We experience peace when we maintain a perspective in our hearts and minds that says, "God is in control." We may not have control over our circumstances; but our loving Heavenly Father does, and we can rest in Him.

What is the opposite of peace? The words *fear* and *distress* come to mind. They may play out as feelings, but fear and distress are really perspectives of the heart and mind as well. Observe David's perspective of peace in Psalm 34:

> I prayed to the LORD, and he answered me,
> freeing me from all my fears.
> Those who look to him for help will be radiant with joy;
> no shadow of shame will darken their faces.
> I cried out to the LORD in my suffering, and he heard me.
> He set me free from all my fears.
> For the angel of the LORD guards all who fear him,
> and he rescues them.
> Taste and see that the LORD is good.
> Oh, the joys of those who trust in him!

Let the LORD's people show him reverence,
>   for those who honor him will have all they need.
Even strong young lions sometimes go hungry,
>   but those who trust in the LORD will never lack any good
>   thing.[17]

Are you willing to take on a new perspective—a perspective of peace? Don't wait for the feeling in order to experience the blessing! As Paul said, "Let the peace that Christ gives control your thinking."[18] May our hearts and minds rest in the Lord, as we trust our lives into His loving hands.

Experiencing True Peace

Have you ever sat for an hour or two by a still pond or relaxed for an afternoon by a lazy river? Those are calm and peaceful surroundings to be sure. But they're not the places where God teaches us peace. If we want to experience true peace, we have to accept the fact that our classroom will most likely be found in the midst of troubles, challenges, and turmoil. Personally I would love to go through life learning only happy lessons from easy instructors, but that's not how the best lessons are learned. Thinking back to my school days, I recall that the easy classes were nice; but the challenging classes were the ones that strengthened me and took me to new heights of knowledge and understanding.

The troubles in our lives may lead us to question God: "Don't You want me to have peace? Why do You allow my life to be so difficult?" I'm sure many of the early Christians had similar questions as they faced persecution of all types. That's why James wrote, "My brothers and sisters, when you have many kinds of troubles, you should be full of joy, because you know that these troubles test your faith, and this will give you patience. Let your patience show itself perfectly in what you do. Then you will be perfect and complete and will have everything you need."[19]

True peace is barely noticeable when we're in calm surroundings, but it shines brightly in our trials and difficulties. In a troubled marriage, when a child goes astray, in the face of cancer or multiple sclerosis or Lou Gehrig's disease, God can cultivate a peace that passes all understanding. We know it's from Him, because it's not dependent upon feelings or circumstances. God's peace goes way beyond anything we can generate within ourselves.

War and Peace

Difficulties and discouragements do not last forever, but God's peace does. There is hope in His help. As we go through life, we may not find peace in every circumstance or relationship; but we can always find it in the Lord. He will give us what we need for the journey.

A friend of mine, Sheri Prescott, knows what it means to have God's peace in the midst of uncertainty. Her husband serves our country in the military, and one week before his deployment to Iraq, Sheri was in a terrible accident. Both bones in her lower right leg were broken. Sheri was confined to a wheelchair for a month and had to use crutches for several more months. With a severely broken leg, a husband deployed halfway around the world, and a toddler to care for at home, you would think that Sheri would have developed a perspective of self-pity, overwhelm, and fear. On the contrary, Sheri chose to see her circumstances as an opportunity to trust God and look to Him for peace. Certainly she needed people to help her, and God provided the help she needed at the time. But here's what she has to say about her faith in God and the peace He has given her:

> My flesh wants to worry about Tony. Negative thoughts come like a flood: Is Tony okay tonight? Could my loving husband be shot and hurting? What would happen to our baby daughter and me? How can I face another day without him? Lord, how could You let him leave me?

I cling to the words in 1 John 4:18 (The Message): "Well-formed love banishes fear. Since fear is crippling, a fearful life—fear of death, fear of judgment—is one not yet fully formed in love."

Because of Jesus' "well-formed" love in me, I do not fear. I will not fear! I choose faith instead of fear. God loves Tony even more than I do. He knew even before we were born that my husband would go off to fight this war with the red, white, and blue beside him. We both face each day knowing that it's not in our hands. It is in our Father's hands. Fear doesn't change our circumstances; it just allows Satan to have a foothold into our minds. Our spirits are renewed by faith . . . yours can be too![20]

Sheri's words remind us that we can live above our circumstances. We can choose to have a perspective of peace and experience the true peace that comes only from God. He is our loving and merciful Heavenly Father. He is the sovereign Lord of the universe. Whatever the circumstances He allows to pass through His loving hands and into our lives, we don't have to deal with them alone. He will surely be with us through them. How wonderful! How freeing! How delightful to live our lives in peace, with our eyes fixed on Him!

Calming Thoughts

Scripture Reading: Psalm 62, "God's Peace"

Quiet Meditations:
- How does this passage encourage a perspective of peace?
- What does this psalm tell you about God?
- What does this psalm tell you about *you*?

Personal Prayer:

Glorious God of peace, I praise You because all things in life are under Your control. You are my Good Shepherd. You tend to my life like a loving shepherd tends his flock. I confess that I am often weak and fearful. I try to create my own peace instead of looking to You. Forgive me, Lord. Thank You for never leaving me. Replace my fear and anxiety with the peace that passes all understanding. Give me Your true peace, even in the midst of life's storms. Help me to rest in Your powerful and loving arms. In Jesus' name I pray, amen.

7

Casting Off Cares versus Cuddling Up with Them

Every evening I turn my worries over to God.
He's going to be up all night anyway.

MARY C. CROWLEY

Cast your cares on the LORD
and he will sustain you;
he will never let the righteous fall.

PSALM 55:22 NIV

There once was a woman who worried all the time about everything. Her friends knew her as a chronic worrier, and her continual fretting was obvious in her forlorn demeanor. One day, to everyone's surprise, she strolled into town, smiling and whistling. Her friends were aghast!

"Can this be our friend?" they whispered. "Surely not, for our friend has a constant look of worry on her face." They could hardly believe they were looking at the same woman. They approached her and asked, "What has happened?"

"Oh, I'm paying another woman to do my worrying for me," she replied.

"You mean you aren't worrying anymore?" her friends inquired.

"No. Whenever I'm inclined to worry, I just let her do it."

"How much do you pay her?"

"Two thousand dollars a week."

"Wow! How can you afford that?" her friends asked.

"I can't, but that's her worry," she blissfully replied.[1]

Hire someone to worry for us? Sounds like a good idea! Just think of the job potential that professional worriers would have in our society today. They'd never be lacking for work; that's for sure!

As Christians we don't have to pay someone to worry for us; we have a Heavenly Father who will do it for free. You may be thinking, *Oh, but I don't want to bother Him with my problems, complaints, and worries.* Here's the amazing truth: Our wonderful, loving God *wants* us to bring our cares and worries to Him. That's His continual plea to us throughout Scripture: "Fear not." "Don't fret." "Don't be anxious." "Cast your cares upon Me." Of course, being free from worry doesn't mean being free from responsibility. God expects us to take action in our circumstances in obedience to Him. Rather, being free from worry means that as we place our cares at God's feet, we don't waste time fretting about things over which we have no control.

Cuddling Cares

Doesn't it seem like somewhere in a mother's job description there should be a line item with the title "Chief Worrier"? I mean, *someone* has to worry about the kids' health and their homework and their friendships and getting the right teachers and what if they don't make the basketball team and where they will go to college and who they will marry and how they will turn out. Phew! With so much to worry about, maybe we should be worried if we aren't worrying!

Actually, it's easy for us to cuddle up on the couch with our worries and cares. We have become a society that is quite comfortable with worry; when given the opportunity, we all tend to gravitate toward it. Yet worry has the tendency to rob us of our joy, hope, and peace. It zaps us of our strength. As someone once said, "Worry is wasting today's time to clutter up tomorrow's opportunities with yesterday's troubles."[2]

Even worse, cuddling our cares is disobedience to God. Have you ever thought about worry in such severe terms? Throughout the Bible, God has commanded us not to worry, because it diminishes our faith and trust in Him. Yet so many of us choose to worry rather than cast our cares on the Lord. E. E. Wordsworth wrote this convicting commentary about worry in the *Gospel Herald*:

> There is a little motto that hangs on the wall in my home that again and again has rebuked me: "Why worry when you can pray?" We have often been reminded of the words of the psalmist, "Fret not thyself because of evildoers, neither be thou envious against the workers of iniquity" (Psalm 37:1). Mr. Wesley used to say that he would just as soon swear as to worry. Worrying is evidence of a serious lack of trust in God and His unfailing promises. Worry saddens, blights, destroys, kills. It depletes one's energies, devitalizes the physical man, and enervates the whole spiritual nature. It greatly reduces the spiritual stature and impoverishes the whole spirit.[3]

Now, now. Don't start worrying about being a worrier! Instead, as you read this chapter and as I write it (yes, I need this message too), let's give ourselves a healthy nudge and get up off that comfy couch. Let's stop cuddling our cares. From this day forward, we can make a conscious decision to replace our worry with prayer. We can choose to cast our cares on the Lord rather than hold on to them like a well-loved, well-worn blanket.

Humble Casting

As a teenager I memorized 1 Peter 5:7 in the King James Version. It says, "Casting all your care upon him; for he careth for you." It was a comforting verse to me, especially during the emotional ups and downs I experienced during those teenage years. The verse could stand on its own and be completely meaningful, enriching, and encouraging to any of us, wherever we are in life; but it doesn't stand by itself. It is actually a continuation of a command in the previous verse.

Some modern translations separate verse 7 from the previous thought, but the New English Translation keeps it intact. Have I piqued your interest? Are you wondering what Peter said prior to the "casting all your care" part? Here it is: "And all of you, clothe yourselves with humility toward one another, because God opposes the proud but gives grace to the humble. And God will exalt you in due time, if you humble yourselves under his mighty hand by casting all your cares on him because he cares for you."[4]

Are you scratching your head? I was too. When I first read this passage, I wondered, *What does humility have to do with casting our cares on the Lord?* Then I began thinking about the opposite of humility, which is pride or arrogance. Pride says, "I can handle this on my own. I can deal with my own cares." Humility says, "I can't do this on my own. I need God."

How easy it is for us as moms to think that we are in control, that we can handle our own challenges! I grieve over the time I have wasted worrying and fretting, when the pride in my heart expressed, "I don't trust Your care for me, God. I'm going to handle this myself." If only I had done more casting and less worrying! Casting our cares on God is an act of humility and humble reverence toward Him. It demonstrates our understanding that (1) He really does care for us, and (2) He can handle our worries and challenges much better than we can. It is, in essence, an act of worship.

Turning Worry into Wonder

Here's a question for you: Is it possible to be carefree? I'm not asking, can we have a life void of challenges and troubles? I'm asking, can we be free from the worry that goes along with life's challenges? According to the apostle Paul, the answer is yes. Paul told the early Christians—who faced tremendous challenges, including persecution and death—that they ought to live a worry-free lifestyle. Here's what he had to say in Philippians chapter 4 (you read the first part of this passage in the previous chapter, but I want you to see the full context):

> Do not worry about anything, but pray and ask God for everything you need, always giving thanks. And God's peace, which is so great we cannot understand it, will keep your hearts and minds in Christ Jesus.
>
> Brothers and sisters, think about the things that are good and worthy of praise. Think about the things that are true and honorable and right and pure and beautiful and respected. Do what you learned and received from me, what I told you, and what you saw me do. And the God who gives peace will be with you.[5]

Notice Paul didn't say, "If you want to, try not to worry about anything, because everything is going to be great." No, he gave a good, hearty command: "Do not worry about anything, but pray and ask God for everything you need." Will there be times in our lives when everything isn't great? Of course. Will worry try to creep back into our hearts and minds? Absolutely. But Paul says, "Don't do it!" Instead, he tells us to immediately go to prayer, then think about the things that are good and pleasing and honorable. In other words, we need to clean out the worry from our hearts and then perfume them with the wonderful truth that God cares for us and is lovingly in control of our lives.

When we are tempted to worry, we can apply the Philippians 4 principle: Pray, then put a new truth into our minds. Through prayer we actively cast our burdens on God. Through a new mind-set, we actively replace our worry with God's Truth. For each care that you have, I encourage you to find a scripture to put in its place. This has been a very helpful practice for me personally. For example, whenever I feel afraid to stand up in front of an audience to give a speech, I cast that care upon the Lord through prayer, then I replace the worry by filling my mind with Joshua 1:9: "Remember that I commanded you to be strong and brave. Don't be afraid, because the LORD your God will be with you everywhere you go."

Here are some other great verses to help you replace worry with wonder:[6]

- Psalm 5:11: "But let all who take refuge in you be glad; let them ever sing for joy. Spread your protection over them, that those who love your name may rejoice in you."
- Psalm 34:4: "I sought the LORD, and he answered me; he delivered me from all my fears."
- Psalm 56:3, 11: "When I am afraid, I will trust in you . . . In God I trust; I will not be afraid. What can man do to me?"
- Psalm 91:4: "He will cover you with his feathers, and under his wings you will find refuge; his faithfulness will be your shield and rampart."
- Proverbs 3:5–6: "Trust in the LORD with all your heart and lean not on your own understanding; in all your ways acknowledge him, and he will make your paths straight."
- Isaiah 41:10: "So do not fear, for I am with you; do not be dismayed, for I am your God. I will strengthen you and help you; I will uphold you with my righteous right hand."
- Jeremiah 17:7: "But blessed is the man who trusts in the LORD, whose confidence is in him."
- John 14:1: "Do not let your hearts be troubled. Trust in God; trust also in me [Jesus]."

Why not write several of these verses down on index cards and place them in strategic places? For instance, if you tend to worry about your kids each day after you drop them off at school, put a scripture card on the dashboard of your car to remind yourself to turn those cares over to God. If you are worried because you have a significant role to play in an upcoming event, put a scripture card with your file of notes and papers for the event to remind yourself to keep things in perspective. If you are worried about a certain plan you have for the future, put a faith-filled scripture card directly on your calendar. No matter what your concern, you can turn your troubled mind toward truthful thinking by dwelling on scriptures from God's Word.

Kicking Cares Out

Several years ago we bought a puppy. She was so cute and huggable that my husband and I agreed to allow her to sleep on our bed with us at night. I should probably mention that our lovable pooch is an English mastiff named Abbey. If you know anything about English mastiffs, you know that they start off small, but they can grow to weigh as much as 150 to 200 pounds. Abbey currently tilts the scales at 165.

Abbey started off as a sweet little bedmate. As she grew, however, so did her annoying tendencies, such as snoring, hogging the covers, and waking us up every time she turns over. It's not so easy to get her out of the bed anymore. She jumps up while we're asleep, and when we try to get her off the mattress, she becomes a dead weight. It's a constant "bed battle."

Worry, on the other hand, is a constant "head battle." It may start out as a cuddly little care; but if we allow it to linger, it can grow into full-blown worry and despair. Stay vigilant! Don't let cares and worries make their home in your head. Instead, begin the practice of casting your cares on God, because He genuinely cares for you. Start by being humble, recognizing your need for God. Then continually give your cares, concerns, and worries to Him through prayer. Finally, replace your worry with wonder by filling your mind with the truth of Scripture.

As moms, let's not waste another minute cuddling up to our cares. Let's cast them off on our loving Heavenly Father and discover the peace that comes from putting our trust in Him.

Calming Thoughts

Scripture Reading: Psalm 30 and Psalm 56:3–4, "God Cares for Us"

Quiet Meditations:
- How did the psalmist deal with problems, struggles, and worries in his life?
- What are some of the cares and worries that you're cuddling in your life right now?
- Are you willing to turn those worries over to God and leave them with Him, trusting Him to be your rock and your protector?

Personal Prayer:
Loving Father, I praise You for Your wonderful care for me. Thank You for wanting me to bring my concerns and worries to You. You are willing and able to handle them much better than I can! I confess that I often hold on to my worries instead of giving them over to You. I humbly recognize my need for You. Help me to cast my cares on You, and teach me to replace my worries with Your Word of Truth. I put every area of my life into Your loving hands. Help me to rest in the fact that You are good and can be trusted. In Jesus' name I pray, amen.

8

Delicious Daily Morsels
of God's Word

How precious is the Book divine,
By inspiration given!
Bright as a lamp its doctrines shine,
To guide our souls to heaven.

JOHN FAWCETT

Do not let this Book of the Law depart from your mouth;
meditate on it day and night, so that you may be careful to
do everything written in it. Then you will be prosperous and
successful.

JOSHUA 1:8 NIV

Lately I've started a daily ritual of enjoying afternoon tea. Almost every day around 3:00 p.m., I put the kettle on the stove and take a minibreak from my responsibilities. It gives me a little lift and something to look forward to in the middle of a busy day. I've gotten to the point where I feel slightly disappointed if I'm not at home and I miss my delightful tea time.

Funny how we get attached to certain rituals. For me, they're usually food related. Other women may enjoy watching *Oprah* or working out or calling a friend or taking a short nap every afternoon. Somehow we find consolation in these regular practices, and we do our best to keep them up and not let anything get in their way.

Sipping tea, working out, stopping to watch a certain TV show every day—all of these routines can have redeeming value. They can help reduce our levels of daily stress. But there is one habit or routine that has a multitude of benefits, far beyond those of tea drinking or power walking. What routine is that? I'm referring to the routine of taking in a daily dose of God's Word. Delicious morsels of Scripture can strengthen us, inspire us, teach us, convict us, and guide us.

Wow! With all those benefits, you'd think we would make reading the Word our number one daily ritual. But many of us don't. I must humbly admit that I've had days when I was more disappointed over missing my tea than missing my daily Bible study. Can you relate?

Better Than Chocolate

The Bible speaks to our hearts like no other book. It offers sweet, delicious refreshment and powerful nourishment for our spirits. The dynamic nineteenth-century preacher Samuel Chadwick put it eloquently when he said, "I have worked over the Bible, prayed over the Bible for more than sixty years, and I tell you there is no book like the Bible. It is a miracle of literature, a perennial spring of wisdom, a wonderful book of surprises, a revelation of mystery, an infallible guide of conduct, an unspeakable source of comfort."[1]

What delicacies await us when we open the Bible! Do you want to nourish your spirit and experience true joy and peace? Do you want to hear God's voice and know His will for your life? Then sit at His table and feed on His divinely-inspired Word. It's spiritual food for the soul. Here's what the apostle Paul wrote about the power of Scripture in his second letter to Timothy:

Since you were a child you have known the Holy Scriptures

which are able to make you wise. And that wisdom leads to salvation through faith in Christ Jesus. All Scripture is given by God and is useful for teaching, for showing people what is wrong in their lives, for correcting faults, and for teaching how to live right. Using the Scriptures, the person who serves God will be capable, having all that is needed to do every good work.[2]

Think about it this way: Not only is food a pleasure to eat, but without it we would grow weak and eventually die. We need food as fuel to support the proper functioning of our bodies. Can you imagine a friend saying to you, "Hey, I ate a little bit of food on Sunday morning, so why do I need to eat again? I'll just wait until next Sunday." I don't know about you, but I enjoy food too much to eat just once a week. Besides, if I had only one meal a week for the rest of my life, the rest of my life wouldn't last very long!

Most of us do a good job of eating enough food to satisfy our hunger and keep our bodies running. But what about our spirits? We wouldn't think of purposely depriving our bodies of physical food, yet many of us starve our spirits of spiritual food. We allow the cares and responsibilities of our daily lives to crowd out the time we need to feed on God's Word. It's easy to think, *I read a little bit of the Bible at church on Sunday. That ought to carry me through the rest of the week.* Not true! As one church billboard read, "Seven days without Bible study and prayer makes one weak."

Just as we have regular mealtimes to feed ourselves and our families, we also need to have regular times to feed our spirits with Scripture. When is a good time for you to pull up to the table and take in some Good News? You can start with something as simple as a daily ten-minute devotional. The point is to begin to establish a routine (just like my afternoon tea). As you begin to feed on God's Word, you will soon find your appetite for Scripture increasing. Go ahead and indulge yourself! When it comes to the Bible, it's okay to overeat.

My Personal Favorites

If you're new to Bible study, you may be saying to yourself, *But there are so many different versions and editions of the Bible. How do I know which one to read?* I have personally grown fond of several different versions. Now mind you, I don't have a degree from a theological seminary, so I'm not a biblical scholar; but I do love God's Word. It's on that basis that I want to share with you a few of the Bibles I find useful for my own personal study. Perhaps my list of favorites will help you choose a version that is right for you. Or, if you already have a favorite Bible, perhaps you'll find an additional version that can supplement your current reading and study:

- *The One Year Chronological Bible*, New International Version (Tyndale House, 1995). This volume offers 365 daily readings of the Bible arranged sequentially, in the order the events actually occurred. For instance, one daily reading may include a reading from the Book of Psalms, along with a passage in 2 Samuel that describes the event that motivated David to write the psalm. Reading the stories in the Old and New Testaments in their correct chronological order increases my understanding of the context of each story. This is a great Bible for daily readings.
- *The NET Bible*, New English Translation (Biblical Studies Press, 2003). The NET Bible, created to be the first major modern English translation available free for download on the Internet for personal and group Bible study, is available in its entirety on the Web at www.netbible.com. A new approach to translation, it is thoroughly documented with over sixty thousand notes by translators and editors explaining why they chose to translate words or phrases in certain ways and what their alternatives were. This is a tremendous text for an accurate word study of the Bible.

- *Life Application Study Bible*, New Living Translation (Tyndale House, 1996). This revised version of the Living Bible is considered a general purpose translation that is accurate, easy to read, and excellent for study. *The Life Application Study Bible* provides study helps, time lines, maps, charts, commentaries, overviews, cross references, a dictionary, and a concordance, all in one single-bound edition. I find it very helpful for general reading and study.

- *The Word Becomes Flesh*, New Century Version (Thomas Nelson, 2005). This is a complete audio rendition of the New Testament read by a variety of women from all walks of life. The New Century text is both accurate and clear, and the audio format engages listeners with the power of the spoken word. It offers a tremendous way to fill your mind with God's Truth while you travel in the car or do your morning workout.

- *Comparative Study Bible*, New International Version, The Amplified Bible, King James Version, and the Updated New American Standard Bible (Zondervan, 1999). This big Bible has four translations side by side, so you can examine a scripture in four different versions on the same page. This book is a valuable resource when I am seeking to gain a well-rounded understanding of a particular passage in Scripture. Reading a passage in four different translations increases my comprehension and gives me a broader perspective on the text.

- *Talk Thru the Bible* by Bruce H. Wilkinson and Kenneth Boa (Thomas Nelson, 1997). This easy-to-use handbook is a wonderful reference tool. Filled with charts, illustrations, and outlines, it summarizes each book of the Bible and helps explain its historical context as well as its place in Scripture as a whole. I recommend keeping this book next to your Bible for reference.

Numerous devotionals, study guides, concordances, and commentaries are available to supplement your Bible reading and assist you in your study. I won't recommend certain ones here; you will want to find books that suit your own needs and interests. I encourage you to visit your local Christian bookstore and check out what it has to offer. You'll find helpful people there who can lead you to the devotionals and study guides that best fit your needs.

Spiritual Vitamins

The late, great author Catherine Marshall wrote about the danger of "malnutrition of the spirit" in her book *A Closer Walk*. This book is actually a compilation of some of her personal journal entries and was published after she died. She began the following entry by describing the challenge she faced as the new mom of three young children:

> The problems that arise in second marriages are more than I could ever have imagined. Being a new mother to three young children is exhausting, leaving little time for creative writing. There are times when life seems to go gray; I have no zest for anything. When this happened last week I recognized my problem: malnutrition of the spirit.
>
> It was Carol, my friend from California, who had made me aware months ago that spiritual undernourishment can be quite as real as physical starvation. When I first met Carol, it was obvious that she had problems, but not the usual ones. She had a happy marriage; no major troubles with her three children; everything fine economically; no health difficulties.
>
> But she felt tired all the time from the daily routine. "Nothing is much fun anymore," she had said. "I have so little energy that no undertaking seems worth attempting. What's wrong with me?"
>
> An hour and much talk later, I had a sudden inspiration: Could it be that Carol's inner spirit was starving to death? . . .

"We have three meals a day," I suggested. "Perhaps we need spiritual food three times a day too."

"But what is spiritual food? And how do you take it?" Carol asked.

"Jesus said that His words are spirit and life indeed. He used metaphor upon metaphor to tell us that His Spirit is our life substance. He described Himself as 'living water' and 'the bread of life.' Meeting Him in Scripture is like an intravenous feeding from His Spirit to our spirit," I replied.

"So," I challenged Carol, "would you be willing to try spiritual food in the form of life-giving Bible verses three times a day for one month?"

At a Christian bookstore Carol found an "Inspiration Box" of paper capsules, each containing a verse of scripture. They were to be taken daily as spiritual vitamins. (This word "vitamin" means "life substance.")

Later, with another spiritually undernourished friend, we decided that an additional blessing came when we took the time ourselves to dig through Scripture and put together a homemade card file of spiritual vitamins.

So last week I produced a "Vitamin Box" of dozens of favorite passages for my new family. I used a concordance and looked up words such as *strength, food, bread, water, hunger,* and *thirst.* Other cards were culled from Christ's own words. Now before blessing the food at each meal, we pass the box, and one of the children chooses a card to read aloud. The nourishment is most effective when the life-giving words of Scripture are memorized and so become the permanent possessions of mind and heart.

Catherine then wrote down several of her favorite verses. She concluded her journal entry with these words:

By saturating my mind with these and other verses, I find that the grayness lifts, the spirit is infused with spiritual food, and I am ready to meet any difficulty that comes along.[3]

You and I need to have our spirits infused too. As women and as moms, we desperately need the spiritual refreshment and nourishment found only in the frequent, regular intake of God's powerful Word. Without an adequate dose of spiritual vitamins, our lives become gray and our spirits shrivel. We become less calm and more stressed. So let's commit together to feed upon Scripture. Let's make it our satisfying daily bread, allowing it to teach us, guide us, strengthen us, and bring us peace. May our prayers echo the prayer of the psalmist: "Revive me by your word"![4]

Calming Thoughts

Scripture Reading: Psalm 119:1–112, "Food for the Soul"

Quiet Meditations:
- Underline the verses in this passage that show the psalmist's love and delight for God's Word.
- What are some of the benefits of knowing and meditating upon God's Word or law?
- Do you read God's Word as daily nourishment? If not, consider making it a part of your regular routine. Determine when and where you will have your Bible study, and keep that commitment.

Personal Prayer:
I praise You, Father, because Your Word is perfect. Thank You for providing words of life to strengthen and guide me. You are so good to me! I confess that I often let activities and interests get in the way of reading the Bible. I forget how much I need its spiritual nourishment. Revive me by Your Word, O God! Help me to be intentional about reading Scripture daily and enjoying its blessings. Lead me to apply its principles to my life. Thank You that Your Word is a lamp to my feet and a light to my path. In Jesus' name I pray, amen.

three

Renew Your Body

A healthy body is a guest chamber for the soul.

FRANCIS BACON

Or don't you know that your body is the temple of the Holy Spirit, who lives in you and was given to you by God? You do not belong to yourself, for God bought you with a high price. So you must honor God with your body.

1 CORINTHIANS 6:19–20 NLT

Our physical well-being is an important factor in creating a calm spirit. As we renew our bodies, we strengthen our ability to handle stress.

9

Increasing the
"Happy Hormones"

There is no duty so much underrated as the duty of being happy.

ROBERT LOUIS STEVENSON

A happy heart is like good medicine,
but a broken spirit drains your strength.

PROVERBS 17:22

Cindy had the blues. With tears streaming down her face, she tried to find the words to explain her cloudy mood to her husband, but all she could say was that she just felt low. Been there?

Most women know what it's like to feel the blues now and then. "Minor swings into depression or anxiety are very common" for women, says Susan Nolen-Hoeksema, professor of psychology at the University of Michigan in Ann Arbor.[1] The good news is we can ward off the blues—or at least lessen their effect. Yes, there actually are steps we can take to increase our feelings of happiness!

Before we get to those steps, however, let's clarify one point: Happiness is different than joy. Happiness is a cheerfulness that may fluctuate with circumstances or mood. Joy is more of a constant; it's an inner strength that flows from the delight, peace, and contentment we have in the Lord. In chapter 1, we learned about the deep delight we can experience in a relationship with God. It's entirely possible, however, to have joy in our hearts yet not feel happy on the surface. The question is, How can we decrease the clouds in our lives—the things that tend to overshadow us and make us blue physically—so that the joy in our hearts can shine through?

In this chapter, we're going to explore ways to increase our cheerfulness physiologically. You see, our bodies and emotions work hand in hand. Dr. Gregory L. Jantz, author of *Moving beyond Depression*, speaks of the relationship between physical and emotional health. "Few people realize the impact their physical state has on their ability to overcome depression," he says. "Depression is not a mental condition but a debilitating whole-body condition that must be addressed physically as well as mentally."[2] Please understand, this chapter is *not* offered as a definitive solution for depression. But we can increase our "happy hormones" to a certain extent by making a few simple lifestyle changes.

What Are "Happy Hormones"?

The word *hormone* comes from a Greek word meaning "arouse to activity." In His infinite wisdom, God has designed each of us with certain chemicals, or hormones, in our brains that can have an uplifting effect on our moods and emotional states. They're produced by the endocrine glands and secreted into the blood, which carries them to distant cells and organs, stimulating physiological changes within these regions.[3] Of the various hormones that exist in our bodies, two are especially important for the purposes of this chapter.

Serotonin is a type of neurotransmitter that sends messages from one nerve cell to another. Generally speaking, neurotransmitters help different parts of the brain "talk" to each other. Serotonin in particular is involved in numerous body functions such as appetite, mood, hormonal balance, the sleep/wake cycle, and alertness. Alterations in the serotonin level in the brain can be part of the clinical basis for depression, PMS, postpartum blues, and eating disorders.[4] Considered the chemical that helps maintain a "happy feeling," serotonin aids in keeping our moods under control by regulating sleep, calming anxiety, and relieving depression.

Endorphins are a type of chemical called peptides that are produced by the body and released into the brain in response to stress or trauma.[5] As such, they're responsible for making us feel better, improving our moods, increasing our pleasure, and minimizing our pain. You could say they help us achieve a "natural high." Twenty different types of endorphins have been discovered in the nervous system. One of those, betaendorphin, is eighteen to fifty times stronger than morphine in relieving pain. Another endorphin, dynorphin, is thought to be five hundred times stronger. Some scientists claim that in addition to impacting the nervous system, endorphins enhance the immune system, help lower blood pressure, and even produce certain antiaging effects.[6]

What's the point of this little science lesson? Simply this: We don't have to live at the mercy of fluctuating hormones and their accompanying mood swings. There are ways we can naturally lift the levels of serotonin and endorphins in our bodies. With a few simple lifestyle changes, we can actually increase our "happy hormones."

Exercise Away the Stress

"We know that exercise has an antidepressant effect," explains Dr. Bonnie Spring, professor of psychology at the University of Health Sciences/Chicago Medical School. Science proves it: In a study at Texas A&M University College of Medicine, women reported significant improvements in mood after twenty minutes or more of walking.[7] Why? Exercise boosts the body's production of serotonin. Intense, lengthy exercise also increases the release of endorphins, which probably explains the euphoric feeling that athletes commonly refer to as the "runner's high."[8]

To benefit most from these increases in "happy hormones," we need to get thirty minutes or more of moderate exercise five or six days a week. That means making exercise a part of our daily routines. How? Never underestimate the benefit of your own sidewalk or the local park! Simply taking a walk in the sunlight and fresh air can add to your feeling of well-being. You may find it helpful to have a walking buddy, so you can enjoy the fellowship as well as the accountability.

If you have small kids, you can involve them in the process by pushing them in a stroller while you walk. Or you can stay inside and do a simple aerobics tape together in the family room. (One of my favorites is Leslie Sansone's *Walk Away the Pounds*. You can find it at many sporting-goods stores or on the Internet at www.walkawaythe pounds.com.) Another option is to join a health club; many clubs offer childcare programs that give moms a chance to work out while the kids enjoy themselves in separate, supervised play areas. The important thing is to find a form of exercise that suits your current family situation. As one study showed, people who exercise have 1.3 fewer days per month with depressive symptoms than those who do not exercise.[9] So get active, and stay active!

Happy Eating

According to Elizabeth Somer, a registered dietician and author of *Food and Mood* and *Nutrition for Women*, "certain foods or food combinations set off a series of chemical reactions in your brain that help determine whether you feel content, on one hand, or anxious or depressed on the other." If you sense that you're spiraling into depression, Somer suggests eating a snack that combines protein with a carbohydrate; half a turkey sandwich, for example. The combination helps turn on neurotransmitters that naturally invigorate your brain chemicals.

Some people turn to alcohol to alleviate anxiety or depression. Not a good idea, Somer advises, since alcohol is a depressant. "If you're already blue, it will make you feel worse," she says.[10] Dark chocolate, on the other hand, has long been considered an endorphin booster. (Now remember, moderation in all things!)

During low periods, it's wise to gravitate toward foods that contain the amino acid tryptophan, which activates the serotonin in your brain. Foods with tryptophan include turkey, bananas, milk, yogurt, eggs, meat, nuts, beans, fish, and cheese (cheddar, Gruyère, and Swiss). Stay away from simple sugars such as candy, syrups, table sugar, and sweetened fruits; they cause a brief spike in blood sugar that may make you feel better in the short term but can be followed by a quick drop in energy, leaving you craving more.

Two foods to avoid or at least keep at a minimum in your diet are white flour and white sugar, since they require very little energy to metabolize. Because they enter the bloodstream rapidly, they tend to give a quick lift—but then you crash! We'll talk more about sugar and flour in the next chapter. Also avoid foods high in saturated fats (fried foods, for example), because fats inhibit the synthesis of neurotransmitters in the brain.

Vitamin C can be an important addition to your diet, since the conversion of tryptophan into serotonin requires adequate supplies of vitamin C. Other vitamins and minerals can also be helpful in maintaining a feeling of well-being. Some studies show that a deficiency in B-6 or B-12 vitamins can be a contributing factor in depression, for example. Other experts point to magnesium as a depression fighter. Omega-3 fatty acids, found in sources such as fish oil or flax seed oil, can be important too; a diet deficient in these essential acids may lower brain levels of serotonin.

Several herbal remedies have become popular in the past few years for fighting anxiety and depression. St.-John's-wort, for example, contains an ingredient called hypericin, which helps to prevent the chemical processes that destroy serotonin. Kavakava and Ginkgo biloba have been shown to have properties that reduce stress and improve mood. Of course, you should check with your doctor before adding any kind of supplement to your diet, since certain ones can interact with medications you may already be taking.[11]

Attitude Is Everything

Changing your exercise and eating habits is important for boosting your happy hormones on a regular basis. So is changing your attitude. Research now shows that thoughts, emotions, and behaviors all have an impact on body chemistry. Some studies even show that smiling raises the serotonin levels in your brain. Why not practice smiling at other people (starting with your family members) throughout the day? It will be a blessing to them, and it will give you a lift too! And never underestimate the power of laughter, which research has shown releases endorphins into the body. Call up a friend who makes you laugh. Read a funny book. (Personally, I love reading the jokes in *Reader's Digest*.) Watch a family-friendly comedy show on television. Let loose the laughter!

Change your attitude by refocusing your mind. Turn your thoughts to what is good and pure and truthful. (Remember Philippians 4:6–8?) Anger, guilt, and worry will diminish your happy hormones if left unchecked, so don't wallow in regret or anxiety. Confession is good for the soul and also for your state of happiness. Ask forgiveness, forgive, or make things right, and you will feel a big burden lifted. If you are living in sin, turn from it. Often people give in to temptation thinking that doing so will make them happy, when in reality they end up feeling worse. God forgives our sin, but one of the consequences of living in sin is the physiological effects of guilt. Don't let sin steal the happiness God intends for you!

Relax, Refresh, Renew

Here are a few additional ways to increase your happy hormones:

Discover What Relaxes You and Do It

Perhaps it is a bubble bath or a massage or a manicure. Personally, I am rejuvenated when I have some time alone to read. I love those rainy days or Sunday afternoons when I can play some soft classical music and curl up on the couch with my dogs and a good book. I don't get to do it all the time, but quiet reading is something that is totally relaxing for me, and I look forward to it.

Listen to Good Music

Discover the music that creates a sense of relaxation for you. Some kinds of music can soothe your soul, while others can rub you the wrong way emotionally and make you feel tense or angry. Play soothing music in your household, and set the tone for peace. Use pleasant music instead of television for background noise. Studies show that television noise can be a stressor; so if you feel your tension rising, turn off the TV and play soothing music instead.

Get a Good Night's Sleep

Sleep may directly affect serotonin levels. Some research says that consistent sleep patterns are crucial to ensure the most consistent cycling of serotonin, hormones, and other neurotransmitters.[12] "You're especially vulnerable to mood swings when you're sleep-deprived," says Dr. Bonnie Spring. "Get enough sleep, particularly when you know that swings are more probable, like during the week before your period. If you have insomnia, try different remedies until you find what works for you."[13]

As moms it is difficult sometimes to get a good night's rest. Tending to a sick child, rocking a crying baby, or waiting for teenagers to come home can rob us of the effective sleep we need. Do the best you can, knowing that at certain times in your life you may be a bit sleep-deprived. Those times won't last forever. Look for other ways to catch up on sleep. Afternoon power naps, for example, can be wonderfully renewing.

Get Out in the Sun

Sunlight is a definite day brightener (no pun intended). Direct sunlight increases the serotonin and melatonin production in the body. During the fall and winter months, people who leave for work in the dark, work indoors during the daylight hours, and then return home in the dark tend to experience general fatigue and mood swings often associated with depression. Research suggests that at least twenty minutes of direct sunlight a day can help alleviate some of the symptoms. Again, moderation in everything—I don't want to make the dermatologists angry with me!

Seek Professional Help

The truth is depression can be brought on by numerous causes. If you experience continuous symptoms of depression for more than two weeks, see your doctor. Many physical conditions can cause you to feel down, including hypoglycemia, heart disease, anemia, sleep apnea, diabetes, endocrine disorders, allergies, and even dehydration. There can be a heredity component as well.

As we said earlier, this chapter is not intended as a cure-all but rather as an encouragement to explore simple ways you can renew your mind and body. If you need professional help to overcome continuous depression or overwhelming anxiety, by all means, seek out a biblically based counselor.

The Pursuit of Happiness

Ultimately any discussion of the pursuit of happiness must bring us to our need for God. All the remedies and formulas in the world can't fulfill the longing in our hearts for the joy that only God can bring. Our souls' satisfaction is found in God alone. Jesus spoke of this blessed satisfaction in His famous Sermon on the Mount:

> God blesses those who realize their need for him,
>> for the Kingdom of Heaven is given to them.
> God blesses those who mourn,
>> for they will be comforted.
> God blesses those who are gentle and lowly,
>> for the whole earth will belong to them.
> God blesses those who are hungry and thirsty for justice,
>> for they will receive it in full.
> God blesses those who are merciful,
>> for they will be shown mercy.
> God blesses those whose hearts are pure,
>> for they will see God.
> God blesses those who work for peace,
>> for they will be called the children of God.
> God blesses those who are persecuted because they live for
>> God,
>> for the Kingdom of Heaven is theirs.[14]

The word *blessed* in the Bible means more than simply happy. When we recognize our need for God and walk in His ways, we are truly blessed. We're filled with joy! Jesus went on to say, "You are the light of the world—like a city on a mountain, glowing in the night for all to see. Don't hide your light under a basket! Instead, put it on a stand and let it shine for all."[15]

Jesus wants His followers to shine brightly with hearts satisfied in Him. As a Christian, you have a light to shine and a joy to share with the world. Don't dim that light or hide it under a basket by allowing physical circumstances to overshadow you. Instead, begin to take steps to increase your "happy hormones" and decrease the clouds.

Calming Thoughts

Scripture Reading: Psalm 107, "God Lifts Up His People"

Quiet Meditations:
- What words or phrases do you see repeated over and over in this psalm?
- Which words or phrases seem to minister most to you?
- Are you willing to call out to God in your distress and look to Him for direction?

Personal Prayer:

Glorious Creator, magnificent God, I praise You, for You have been good to me! Your love is everlasting, and Your faithfulness extends through all generations. Lord, I confess that sometimes when I am in the pit of despair, I forget to call out to You. I need You. Deliver me from feelings of depression, distress, and anxiety. Show me the steps I need to take to help my body stay healthy and strong, so it can function at its best. Thank You for the way You created me. I am truly awed and amazed at Your greatness. In Jesus' name I pray, amen.

10

The Perfect Diet for the Diet-Impaired Woman

Other men live to eat, while I eat to live.

SOCRATES

I will praise you as long as I live.
I will lift up my hands in prayer to your name.
I will be content as if I had eaten the best foods.
My lips will sing, and my mouth will praise you.

PSALM 63:4–5

Think back to the worst dating experience you ever had. You know, that one date when everything that could go wrong did go wrong. I'll never forget the time I asked a guy to go with me to one of those "girls-ask-guys" dances. The dance hall was hot, so everyone was sweaty, droopy, and in bad moods. The music wasn't that great. And to top it off, when the dance was over and we went to get in my date's car, it wouldn't start. We had to hitch a ride home with one of my friends. You can imagine how much my date enjoyed the evening! The next day he had his car towed to a garage, and the mechanic discovered the problem: Someone had poured sugar into his gas tank as a practical joke. Did you know that a car can't run when it has sugar in the gas tank?

I tell you this story as a humorous reminder that we must be careful what we put in our tanks—and I'm not just talking about cars. Putting quality fuel in a gas tank helps a car run at top performance. Likewise, putting healthy food in our bodies helps each of us function at our highest potential. That's the premise of this chapter: developing a practical, lifetime plan for fueling our bodies that will help us maximize our energy, look our best, and feel great.

Why a diet chapter in a book about creating more calm and less stress? Several reasons. As we read in chapter 9, the foods we eat affect chemicals in our brains that regulate our moods and our ability to handle stress. The foods we eat also affect our health, our stamina, our energy, and our weight. The truth is, in order to maintain calm spirits and bodies that run smoothly, we must fill our tanks with good, healthy fuel.

The Lowdown on Our Intake

Are you low-carb, no-carb, or go-carb? South Beach, Atkins, or Maker's Diet? Dr. Phil, Suzanne Somers, or Larry North? Take your pick! Diet plans and weight-loss programs abound these days. Still there are some nonnegotiable basics concerning healthy eating. A healthy diet is

- A balanced diet containing foods from all the food groups
- Low in saturated fats and refined sugar
- Rich in vitamins, minerals, and fiber

Now that's not too complicated, is it? If it's so simple, then why do you and I (and almost everyone else, for that matter) struggle to eat wisely? The truth is, we like food! We like delicious, tasty food—which often means food that is sugary, fried, fattening, and unhealthy. We also live fast-paced lives that leave us little time to cook, so we end up driving through or ordering out way too much. Some of us eat for reasons other than hunger. Some of us struggle with issues such as self-control. And some of us just love snacks!

Stop for a moment and think about your own situation. What keeps you from healthy eating? Circle the statement (or statements) that apply to you:

- I enjoy eating, and I don't seem to have the will power to stop.
- I love the wrong types of foods.
- I eat for comfort when I'm down or lonely or stressed.
- I'm a habitual snacker.
- I don't have time to eat right, so I eat a lot of fast food.
- I eat at restaurants frequently, and I end up eating large portions.
- I eat at restaurants frequently, and I make unhealthy menu choices.
- I'm hooked on sweets.
- I just don't know which foods are good for me.
- I _____ (you fill in the blank).

We all have slightly different reasons for why we don't eat well. A fad diet that works for millions of other women may not work for us, because we have our own personal motivations for eating the way we do. That's why we need a new approach and a practical plan to change our habits.

A New Lifestyle

Although the title of this chapter uses the words *perfect diet*, the reality is the perfect diet is not a diet at all; it's a lifestyle. Diet plans come and go. Studies now show that people who lose weight on fad diets typically gain it all back within a year. If we want more permanent results, we need to make changes in our eating patterns that will last a lifetime.

Remember, the Lord delights in the details of your life, and that includes your health. Ask God to help you to understand your personal motivation for eating the way you do. Ask Him to give you strength and direction on eating what is right. Self-control is one of the fruits of the Holy Spirit, so ask for His help continually as you go through the process of turning an unhealthy lifestyle into a healthy one.

Notice I said "process." Here's my challenge: Let's agree to incorporate one healthy habit into our lifestyles each month. If we can learn one simple principle a month and really ingrain it into our eating patterns, then we should be in the habit of eating right within seven months.

Seven months? But I want one of those quick diets that makes me slim in seven days. I hear you! The truth is most goals worth pursuing take time. We didn't form bad eating habits in seven days, and it is highly unlikely we will be able to conquer them in seven days. Believe me, the time we put into establishing new eating patterns will be well worth it. Not only will we feel better physically, but we'll feel better about ourselves. We'll also have developed healthier lifestyles that we can teach our children, so they can eat and live in a healthy way for the rest of their lives.

Seven Principles for Healthy Eating and Living

Here are the seven principles I've gleaned from a number of different sources:

1. Eat smaller portions.
2. Drink more water.
3. Don't eat late at night.
4. Eat breakfast.

5.   Think before you eat.
6.   Snack smart.
7.   Use wisdom when eating out.

You may have discovered other principles that you'll want to include in your new lifestyle program. Go ahead and add them to the list. Just be sure to tackle only one principle per month, and work to make that one thing a common practice in your life. I suggest you begin on the first day of a month; then when the month changes, you can move on to the next principle.

As you start on each new principle, write it down on several index cards and place the cards throughout your house as reminders. You may want to put them on your bathroom mirror, by the kitchen sink, in the laundry room, with your calendar or planner, and in the car. You also may want to add one of the following Bible verses as encouragement:

- 1 Corinthians 10:31: "If you eat or drink, or if you do anything, do it all for the glory of God."
- Proverbs 15:24: "Wise people's lives get better and better. They avoid whatever would cause their death."
- Proverbs 3:17 NLT: "[Wisdom] will guide you down delightful paths; all her ways are satisfying."
- Isaiah 58:11 NLT: "The LORD will guide you continually, watering your life when you are dry and keeping you healthy, too. You will be like a well-watered garden, like an ever-flowing spring."
- 1 Corinthians 10:13: "But when you are tempted, [God] will also give you a way to escape so that you will be able to stand it."
- Romans 8:5: "But those who live following the Spirit are thinking about the things the Spirit wants them to do."
- Proverbs 2:11: "Good sense will protect you; understanding will guard you."

If you can, try to memorize one or more of the verses. God's Word is powerful. It can give you the strength you need to stick with the program. Now let's get started!

1. Eat Smaller Portions

Our stomachs are approximately the size of a large fist. Stop right now and make a fist. Take a good, long look at it. Now keep that size in mind as you eat! You don't have to limit yourself to fist-sized portions, but use your fist to gauge the amount of food you eat in order to satisfy yourself. Recognizing that you only need small quantities to fill your stomach will prevent binge eating and help you eat smaller meals more frequently. Eating small quantities of healthy food every few hours will not only fire up your metabolism, it will keep your blood sugar elevated, so you experience fewer mood swings and energy dips.[1]

Let me give you two hints that will increase your chances for success with this principle. First, only place smaller portions on your plate to begin with. This is relatively easy to do at home. At a restaurant, where giant portions are the norm, it's a little harder. When your waiter brings you a large quantity, take your knife and cut the portion down. Scoot the excess over to the side or onto another plate, or immediately put it in a doggy bag to take home later.

Second, eat slowly. If you take more time to chew your food, your small portion will last longer, and you'll assist in the digestion process. Also, the slower you eat, the more time you will give your stomach to signal your brain that you are satisfied. When we wolf down our food, we often ignore or miss that feeling of fullness and end up eating too much.

2. Drink More Water

Sometimes we think we are hungry when we are actually de-hydrated. Drink a glass of water before eating and allow it to hydrate your system. I have found that if I drink water throughout the day, I don't feel quite as hungry. Soft drinks don't have the same effect; they tend to dehydrate our systems and increase our desire for other foods. I know that when I have a Diet Coke, I want chips or popcorn to go with it. When I choose water, however, I tend to eat healthier snacks. I'm not telling you to restrict your beverage intake to water only; but I am saying the more water you drink, the more satisfied your body will be. And since water helps flush toxins out of your body, you will reap other health benefits as well.

3. Don't Eat Late at Night

Nocturnal eating is tempting, but it isn't good for us weight-wise. Debra Waterhouse, a registered dietician and author of *Outsmarting the Female Fat Cell*, says, "Your metabolism and caloric needs are lower at night than at any other time during the day. Your metabolism is fastest in the morning and afternoon, then begins to slow down, with the lowest level at night. When your metabolism is low, your fat cells are most active. So, at night, when your metabolism is low and your caloric intake is high, you are more likely to turn fat cells on for storage and gain weight."[2]

If you must eat dinner late, eat less. When that nighttime urge to snack arises, replace the urge with an activity such as calling a friend, writing a note to someone, or walking the dog. Too much late-night eating will not only pack on the pounds, it will make you less hungry in the morning and perhaps lead you to skip breakfast—which, as we'll learn in the next principle, isn't a good idea.

4. Eat Breakfast

Charles Stuart Platkin, author of *Breaking the Pattern*, writes that "throughout countless interviews with experts, they all agree on one strategy for keeping your mood in tip-top form: Eat breakfast!"[3] When we skip breakfast, we are running our bodies on empty—or on the sludge left over from the day before. No wonder our moods are affected!

We need good fuel to start our day: protein to make us alert and healthy carbohydrates to satisfy our hunger and help us keep our cool.

Skipping breakfast has another disadvantage. When we don't start taking in our day's calories until noon, we are starving by lunchtime and tempted to overeat. You may be thinking, *But I'm simply not hungry in the morning.* Well, if you're eating at night, you may not feel hungry, because very little digestion occurs while you are sleeping. "As soon as you start matching your eating to your metabolism and eat less at night, you'll find that you are hungry in the morning and want to eat," explains Debra Waterhouse.[4]

5. Think before You Eat

When you are about to put that delicious morsel in your mouth, stop and ask yourself, are you really hungry, or are you

- bored and just want to munch on something?
- stressed and need something to calm you down?
- upset or depressed and feel that you need food for consolation?

We need to train ourselves to eat for hunger, not for other reasons. Jesus referred to Himself in terms of bread and water. He wants you to find your heart and soul's satisfaction in Him, not in food that alleviates your hunger temporarily but can't satisfy your deepest longing. Jesus said, "I am the bread of life. He who comes to Me shall never hunger, and he who believes in Me shall never thirst."[5] Bring your hurts, stresses, and frustrations to Him. Don't try to eat away the pain with food!

When we stop to think before we eat, we not only examine *why* we are eating, but *what* we are eating. Let's say you're tempted to eat a slice of thick, rich chocolate cake because it looks so good and you love chocolate. Stop and think to yourself, *I want that cake because I love chocolate; but I'm really not very hungry, and I'm trying to cut down on sweets.* After consideration, if you really want to try some of the cake, take a few slow bites. Enjoy the taste and leave the rest. You don't have to finish the whole thing to enjoy it. Thinking before you eat will not only help you with snacks and desserts; it will make it easier for you to choose smaller portions at mealtimes. I'm not saying we shouldn't enjoy the food we eat. I'm simply suggesting that before we eat, we need to think, examine our motivation, and apply self-control to our response.

6. Snack Smart

Snacking is okay. In fact, it's a good thing—if we do it wisely. As we said earlier, smaller quantities of food eaten more frequently is the best way to increase our metabolism and keep our moods in balance. How can you eat healthier snacks? You begin at the grocery store. Don't buy junk food. Decide on several healthy snacks that you know you will enjoy, and keep a plentiful supply on hand. Nuts, low-fat cheese, fruits, vegetables, whole-wheat toast or cheese toast, yogurt, and whole-grain cereal are all good choices.

Consider bringing healthy snacks with you if you are going to be at work or on the run all day. I've personally had many times when I've been out or busy and haven't had a chance to grab something to eat. When my blood sugar level drops, however, I start to feel a little shaky, or I get irritable or stressed. It's amazing how a small snack of fruit, nuts, or cheese can help me make it through to the next meal—and keep me from being ravenously hungry at that meal!

7. Use Wisdom When Eating Out

Almost fifty cents of every dollar spent on food in America is spent in restaurants, fast-food or quick-serve restaurants, or take-outs. Our society is fast becoming a dining-out instead of dining-in culture. I don't know about you, but it's easier for me to make poor eating choices when I'm eating out. I eat more, and I don't eat the right stuff. So what's the solution? I doubt if any of us are going to stop eating out altogether. So here are a few suggestions:

- Order a starter such as soup or salad (ask for fat-free salad dressing or dressing on the side).
- Stay away from all-you-can-eat buffets.
- Choose a lean meat for your main course and try to avoid sauces with oil, cheese, or mayonnaise.
- Ask for vegetables without added butter or oil.
- Replace fries with vegetables or fruit.
- If you must have a potato, choose a sweet potato; it's more nutritious.
- Choose only low-fat desserts, or simply order decaf coffee.

Now about fast food. When my daughter was in kindergarten, I experienced a sudden weight gain. *What have I been doing differently?* I wondered. Then it dawned on me: Almost every day, after I picked up my daughter from school at noon, we drove through a local fast-food restaurant for lunch. No wonder! I quickly decided it was time to slow down on the fast food and change our habits.

I'm a busy mom too, so I know there are times when fast food is unavoidable. Thankfully, many of the national chains are now offering healthier choices, such as fruit or salad instead of fries and low-fat milk instead of soda. Many of them are also posting the nutritional content of their menu selections on their Web sites. You may want to visit the sites of some of your favorite fast-food restaurants and make a list of their less fatty choices. For instance, a Double Whopper with cheese and mayo at Burger King has 1,010 calories and 67 grams of fat, but their Broiler Chicken Sandwich without mayo is 370 calories and 9 grams of fat. Take some time to discover in advance the best choices for you and your family.

High-Octane Menu

We've looked at seven general principles for eating. Now let's look more specifically at *what* to eat. Fueling your body with the right foods—we'll call it our "high-octane menu"—can provide you with more energy in your day and more spring in your step.

First, let me mention three things we should steer away from in our diets: white or refined sugar, white or refined flour, and partially hydrogenated oils. You will feel better, look better, and perform better if you eliminate or at least reduce your intake of these three foods. Why? Both white flour and white sugar have a high glycemic index, causing spikes and dips in your blood sugar level. They may give you a quick high, but then you crash and need to eat again. Personally I've found that as I've moved away from eating sugar (I still have some now and then), I've lost my craving for sweets, I think more clearly, and I have more energy. Back when I ate more sugary foods, they only made me hungry for more. I'm convinced the best thing I have ever done for myself diet-wise is to nearly eliminate sugar and white flour products from my life. Try it for a week and see how good you feel.

Scientists continue to study the health risks associated with hydrogenated and partially hydrogenated oils. Enough is known at this point, however, to recommend that if you see those words on a food label, eat something else! Although we metabolize these trans-fats the same way we do other fats, research now shows that they can cause hardening of the arteries and raise LDL cholesterol (the bad cholesterol), which may result in an increased risk of heart disease. "Foods that are high in trans-fatty acids tend to be low in fiber and high in calories, sodium, sugar, and artificial ingredients," says Dr. David L. Katz of the Yale School of Medicine. "They are also linked to inflammation, which can damage body tissues, increase the risk of chronic disease, and accelerate aging."[6] That's enough to make me want to stay away from hydrogenated oils! How about you?

So what *should* you eat throughout the day? Here's a general plan:

- Breakfast: Eat complex carbohydrates such as whole-grain breads and cereals along with low-fat proteins such as yogurt, cottage cheese, skim or soy milk, lean meat, or eggs.

- Midmorning snack: Eat fruits, vegetables, nuts, cheese, or yogurt.
- Lunch: Have a turkey sandwich on whole-grain bread, or eat other lean meats, low-fat cheese, soup, and/or a salad. Remember that carbohydrates will raise your serotonin level and make you feel sleepy, so if you have an important event in the afternoon and you need to stay focused, gear your menu more toward low-fat protein.
- Afternoon snack: Have cheese and whole-wheat crackers, peanut butter, or vegetable sticks.
- Dinner: Eat raw or steamed vegetables; lean meats such as chicken, fish, or turkey; and whole-grain breads.

It's Simple!

We can sum up a healthy lifestyle in one simple phrase: "Eat right and exercise." In the last chapter, we talked in part about the importance of starting a regular exercise routine. In this chapter, we've added important principles for healthy, high-octane eating. For optimal health, the two really must go hand in hand. Stay committed to a routine of exercise as you implement your healthy eating plan, and you are bound for success. May God give you strength and direction as you honor Him with your body!

Calming Thoughts

Scripture Reading: Psalm 139, "God Knows Everything about You"

Quiet Meditations:
- How does this passage help you feel confident about who you are?
- What does David say specifically about the way you are made?
- Are you willing to allow God to examine your heart and lead you?

Personal Prayer:
Glorious Lord, I praise You, for You are the Creator of all the universe. Not only did You make the sun, the stars, and the earth, You even formed my body in my mother's womb! I praise You for Your wonderful handiwork. You make no mistakes. I confess I haven't always valued my body and taken care of it as I should. I know that my body is where Your Holy Spirit dwells. Help me to be faithful to take care of myself physically, and give me the self-control to eat wisely. Help me to develop a healthy lifestyle that glorifies You. In Jesus' name I pray, amen.

four

Roll with the Punches

'Tis easy enough to be pleasant
When life flows along like a song;
But the man worthwhile
Is the man who will smile
When everything goes dead wrong.

ELLA WHEELER WILCOX

I have learned to be content whatever the circum-
stances.

PHILIPPIANS 4:11 NIV

We may not have control over our circumstances, but
we do have a choice as to how we will adapt and
respond to our circumstances.

Thankfully we know the One who is in control,
and He provides calm in the midst of the storm.

11

"Flexible" Is
My Middle Name

The bamboo which bends is stronger
than the oak which resists.

JAPANESE PROVERB

People may make plans in their minds,
but the LORD decides what they will do.

PROVERBS 16:9

When was the last time you had your day all figured out, but then circumstances completely reshuffled your plans? Maybe a child woke up sick and had to stay home from school; a friend called needing to talk through a difficult emotional issue; a repair man showed up late and took too long. Whatever the case, something unexpected happened, and your best-laid plans went right out the window.

Or maybe you've had to deal with more than a few messed-up days. Maybe the circumstances in your life have reshuffled not only your plans but your *dreams.* A child with a long-term illness, a divorce, a financial crisis that forced you to go back to work—whatever the circumstances, you feel as if life has thrown you a major curve ball.

Wouldn't it be lovely if we could spend our days walking down a clear, straight path toward our life dreams? Unfortunately, that's not realistic. In real life, change happens. I wish it didn't, but it always does. That means if we want to lead lives of more calm and less stress, we need to learn to adjust and adapt. More than that, we need to learn to be flexible and leave any tendency toward grumbling behind.

When I was a junior-high math teacher, I taught my students that the shortest distance between two points is a straight line. I taught equations with numbers that fit into perfect formulas. In life, however, God rarely takes us on the shortest path from A to B. His equations don't always fit into a perfect A + B = C formula. Why? Because He has a bigger overall plan for our lives than we know, and His equations serve a greater purpose than simply solving our day-to-day problems.

God says, "My thoughts are not like your thoughts. Your ways are not like my ways. Just as the heavens are higher than the earth, so are my ways higher than your ways and my thoughts higher than your thoughts."[1] Whether our plans change due to circumstances beyond our control or because of choices we make, we can rest assured that God has a greater plan and purpose for our lives—and it hasn't changed. He will use all the complex variables in our lives to create a unique and beautiful formula that is sure to complete His perfect plan.

Flexibility Is a Choice

The fifth-century Greek historian Herodotus wrote, "There is nothing permanent except change."[2] Change is inevitable. The question is, how will we handle it? Will we adapt, or will we fall apart? Will we find joy in the process, or will we grumble and complain, making everyone miserable along with us? The choice is ours.

Reflect for a moment on your typical response to changes in plans. How would you describe yourself?

- "I adapt easily to changes in plans."
- "I adapt to changes but grumble and complain about them."
- "I get angry when things change, but I get over it quickly."
- "I get angry when things change, and I take it out on the people around me."
- "I completely lose it when my plans are disrupted."
- "I continually fear the possibility of change or crisis in my life."

Did you see yourself in any of those statements? We all react a little differently to change, often because we have different personalities. Some personality types tend to resist change, while others are more easygoing.

My mother, for example, had a melancholy personality. She was very organized and had her ducks in a row at all times. Her well-laid plans were a blessing to us all. The downside to being very precise, however, is that it's hard to adjust when plans change. Don't get me wrong; Mom handled things well, but she was resistant to change simply because she was so organized. Then there's my dad, who is a successful businessman and a creative thinker. When situations change abruptly, he thrives. He sees change as an opportunity to learn and grow, and he takes the challenge head-on. God uses all types in the kingdom of God, of course; but people with more resistance-prone personalities may need to work harder than others to maintain a flexible attitude in life.

You see, being flexible means more than just adapting or adjusting; it means adapting or adjusting without grumbling, complaining, or losing our tempers with our families. Flexibility begins in our minds, moves to our hearts, and flows out through our actions. As William J. Johnson said, "The most significant change in a person's life is a change of attitude. Right attitudes produce right actions."[3]

Essentially, flexibility is a choice—a choice to renew our minds in a way that displays our trust in God. Paul tells us, "Do not be conformed to this present world, but be transformed by the renewing of your mind, so that you may test and approve what is the will of God—what is good and well-pleasing and perfect."[4] By choosing to be flexible, we choose to believe that, whatever the circumstances, God has our lives in His loving hands.

How do we do this, practically speaking? We begin by reflecting on the goodness of God. We say to ourselves, "This is not what I planned, but I look forward to seeing how God will work through this new plan." In other words, we turn the focus of our minds and thoughts toward God rather than the circumstances. After all, whatever happens in our lives is no surprise to God. We may be surprised by our circumstances, but He's not. When change comes, then, we can take a deep breath, gather the facts we need in order to act responsibly, look for the good in the situation, and place our fears and anxieties in His hands.

It's not enough, however, to say with our minds, "I trust God in this situation." We must believe it in our hearts. We must come to the point where our *hearts* say, "I believe in Your love and goodness, Father, and I will trust You through this. I believe You are with me and will never leave me." Then we must rest in the calm assurance of His peace and grace.

In the Old Testament Book of Deuteronomy, we read about a time when the Israelites faced a major change in leadership. Moses was passing on his role as leader of the Israelites to his second-in-command, Joshua. No doubt many of the people felt confused, uncertain, and fearful. But Moses encouraged the Israelites' faith with these words: "Do not be afraid or discouraged, for the LORD is the one who goes before you. He will be with you; he will neither fail you nor forsake you."[5] We can take those words to heart today, just as the Israelites did thousands of years ago. And just as the Israelites believed and then followed Joshua across the Jordan River, we, too, can take action once we know in our minds and believe in our hearts that God is in control. Action follows naturally.

What does flexibility look like in action terms for you and me? We can't really draw a single picture, because situations vary; but generally speaking, we can identify some of the positive attributes of a flexible mom:

- A flexible mom is kind with her words.
- A flexible mom is gentle in her tone.
- A flexible mom takes positive action to move in the right direction.
- A flexible mom thinks before she acts.
- A flexible mom gets the help she needs.
- A flexible mom does not grumble or complain.

Of course, none of us can live up to that description 100 percent of the time. My point in sharing this list is not to discourage you with an impossible goal but rather to give you characteristics you can aspire to achieve through God's grace and strength. When life changes, you can look to God and pray, "Lord, I know You have allowed this situation. I believe You have a bigger plan. I believe You love me and are holding my hand right now. Please give me Your strength to stay calm. Give me Your peace, so that I don't scream, grumble, or shrink back in fear."

I think it would be helpful for us to summarize the progression that leads to flexibility:

1. Change happens.
2. The mind reflects.
3. The heart believes.
4. Actions respond.

According to the Bible, we can be confident that God causes everything (disappointments, changes in plans, wrong decisions, crises) to work together for the good of those who love God and are called according to His purpose for them.[6] When change happens, we can believe with our minds and our hearts that our wonderful Heavenly Father has our lives in His hands. We can rejoice in that knowledge, and then we can live out our faith in calm flexibility!

Joy in the Detours

Not long ago, after speaking at a church in the Dallas area, I met a woman named Laura Nelson. She is a wife and mother of three beautiful children, an active member of her church, and a dedicated community volunteer. I immediately liked her smile and vivacious spirit. When she came up to me after my talk, I could see that this was a mom who had learned by God's grace to adapt to her circumstances in a victorious way. I'll let her tell you her story in her own words:

Parenting is a humbling experience. I've uttered those words to my friends many times, with the emphasis changing from humor to comfort to desperation, depending on the day. The interesting thing about being humbled is that it teaches you about yourself. I believe that our Father in heaven sends us these opportunities for us to learn and grow. He has given me three such opportunities in my children (four, if you count my husband!).

My oldest child has Asperger's Syndrome, a condition that makes it difficult for her to understand social cues and interact with other children in a typical manner. While her case is considered mild, one of the many symptoms of AS is emotional volatility. Angry outbursts, obsessive thoughts and worries, and anxiety about things that other children her age wouldn't even notice are all matters we deal with on a daily basis. Add to this two energetic younger brothers who, stereotypically, like loud, rough play, and you have a recipe that can often lead to emotional explosions.

Despite this often-chaotic, noisy world, I prefer to focus on the gifts we have been given through our daughter. We have learned to listen more carefully, love more gently and without condition, and praise more specifically. We have also learned to celebrate milestones that are insignificant to others. Small steps toward conquering fears are encouraged and cheered. Because AS kids tend to be a bit younger emotionally than their peers, we've had more time with the Tooth Fairy, Santa Claus, and the Easter Bunny.

We've also silently cheered the early signs of growing up—the need for privacy, the interest in clothes, and the sounds of pop music coming from her room. When I think of all the gifts I have been given through my experience, I am overwhelmed with gratitude.[7]

Gratitude? Yes, Laura has gratitude, even in her difficulties. Her current life as a mom isn't the road she mapped out for herself as a younger woman, but she has found joy in the detour. That's flexibility: finding joy in the detours of life. The apostle Paul, who experienced many detours in his own life, reminds us, "Always be joyful. Keep on praying. No matter what happens, always be thankful, for this is God's will for you who belong to Christ Jesus."[8]

We have no guarantee what tomorrow may bring, but we do know that God is in control. He holds us in His hands. We can remain flexible, not because we are in charge of our circumstances, but because we trust in our loving God, who cares about the details of our lives. I wish I could tell you the author of the following poem, entitled "He Maketh No Mistakes." The message is profound; the author, unknown:

> My Father's way may twist and turn,
> My heart may throb and ache.
> But in my soul I'm glad I know,

He maketh no mistake.
My cherished plans may go astray,
My hopes may fade away,
But still I'll trust my Lord to lead,
For He doth know the way.
Tho' night be dark and it may seem
That day will never break,
I'll pin my faith, my all in Him,
He maketh no mistake.
There's so much I cannot see,
My eyesight far too dim,
But come what may, I'll simply trust
And leave it all to Him.
For bye and bye the mist will lift,
And plain it all He'll make.
Through all the way, tho' dark to me,
He maketh not one mistake![9]

Calming Thoughts

Scripture Reading: The Book of Ruth, "A Life of Twists and Turns"

Quiet Meditations:

- What major changes did Ruth and Naomi experience in their lives?
- In what ways did God orchestrate Ruth's circumstances? What circumstances led to her meeting Boaz?
- Are you willing to trust God with the twists and turns in your life?

Personal Prayer:

I praise You, Sovereign Lord of the universe! You are the High King of Heaven, and I worship You. I confess that it is easy for me to want to control my own circumstances. But You, O Lord, are the One who is in control. Help me to recognize Your presence when things go the way I plan—and when they don't. Develop a God-centered flexibility in my mind and heart. May I honor You by showing flexibility in my words and actions. In Jesus' name I pray, amen.

12

Seeing Life through the Bright Glasses of Hope

*There is one thing which gives radiance to everything.
It is the idea of something around the corner.*

G. K. CHESTERTON

*Be glad for all God is planning for you. Be patient in
trouble, and always be prayerful.*

ROMANS 12:12 NLT

Michelle Price was a lively little girl from a loving Christian family who climbed trees, rode horses, skied, told far-out stories, and loved to sing. Her life was wonderfully carefree until she was eight years old. That's when her right leg became swollen and started to hurt. After a doctor ran tests, he told Michelle's parents that their daughter had a deadly form of bone cancer. He said Michelle's chances of living were less than 4 percent and that most of her leg would have to be removed right away.

Her parents dreaded telling Michelle the news. When they did, her response was heartbreaking. "Oh, Daddy, I won't be able to dance anymore if I don't have my leg!" she cried. "I don't want to be a cripple." She sobbed for a few minutes. But then she saw her mother's tear-streaked face. She stopped crying, took a deep breath, and said, "I'm going to be okay, Mommy. Don't cry anymore." Patting her mother's face, she continued, "I was scared when Daddy told me, but Jesus made me feel safe inside. I'm going to be all right. You'll see."

Michelle calmly asked her father why God had let this happen. When he said he didn't know, she thought for a few minutes before speaking again. "Maybe I know," she said. "If they don't have any medicine to fix this kind of sickness yet, maybe they can study my leg and find some. Then they can help other kids when they get sick."

The doctors removed Michelle's leg about four to five inches above the knee. She cried when she first looked down at the bandage. Then she told her mom how frightened she had been before going to sleep in the operating room—until she remembered she wasn't alone. Jesus was there with her.

Michelle had intense phantom pains for a while. The nerve endings in her partially removed leg kept telling her brain that something was wrong, resulting in severe pain. Yet, three days after her surgery, Michelle surprised her doctor by joking about her stump and drawing a happy face on the bandage. The doctor told her parents that it normally took amputees a few weeks before they could make themselves even look at their missing part.

Five days after the surgery, the doctors started giving Michelle chemotherapy—powerful drugs designed to kill cancer cells. Because the bone cancer was so deadly, they gave her a dose a thousand times greater than usual. Soon the drugs made all her hair fall out. Each treatment made her extremely sick. She vomited and got such horrible chills that her body shook the bed. But whenever anyone came in and asked how she was feeling, she would say, "Doing okay." She didn't want anyone else to feel badly on her account.

After four weeks in the hospital, she was allowed to go home for a few days. When she went outside with her dad, she realized that the neighbors were uncomfortable around her because of her missing leg and bald head. To make them feel better, she went one by one to her neighbors' homes, told them about her cancer, and invited them to ask questions.

Michelle had chemotherapy on and off for eighteen months and showed great bravery through all the pain and discomfort. When she felt better, she started visiting other children in the hospital who had cancer and tried to cheer them up. Tests showed that her own cancer was gone, and she was filled with thankfulness. In time she learned to ride a skateboard, play soccer using crutches, and ski with one leg. She even won several medals at a national skiing contest for handicapped people. Afterward, on national television, singer Wayne Newton gave her a special sports award for courage. Impressed at how much time Michelle spent trying to make others happy, the entertainer surprised her with a special birthday present: her own horse.

Michelle once told her mom she sometimes felt bad when she was picked last for a sports team or when she wondered if boys would like her, since she only had one leg. Then she added, "I feel bad about feeling bad. God's going to think I'm not grateful for what He's done. I think I'm looking at the bad too much and not enough at what's good."

As she got older, Michelle became the youngest world-class handicapped skier, a fashion model, an inspirational speaker, and one of the top disabled horse riders in the country. She went to college and then worked in a center that helps amputees. In 1993 she was given an award for courage by the American Cancer Society. Today Michelle is a young wife and mother who dreams of someday starting a camp for disabled kids, where she can help teach them about having a positive attitude.[1]

Anyone who knows Michelle's story can't help but admire her. Despite her illness and the loss of her leg, she chose hope over despair. She chose to look up instead of down when life's circumstances were not pretty. We may not be facing a life-threatening cancer or a debilitating handicap, but we all face struggles of different sorts. I don't know about you, but my attitude and resolve are strengthened just by reading about Michelle!

Choice of View

What kind of glasses are you wearing, figuratively speaking? In other words, how do you choose to view your circumstances? Every day we have a choice: Will we look at our lives through the dark glasses of despair, or will we see our world through the bright glasses of hope? It's so easy—even natural—to put on dark glasses and view our troubles with worry, pessimism, and despair. It takes faith, patience, and strength to remove those dark glasses and put on brighter ones.

When we do, though—when we view our world through eyes of hope—we see things a little differently. We recognize that although our circumstances may be difficult, God has not left us. We understand that He will hold us up through our struggles and strengthen us through the dark times.

The early Christians of the Bible lived in uncertain times. Many were persecuted and killed for their faith in Christ. But Paul gave his fellow Christians a message of encouragement and hope. He told them where to put their focus:

> So we do not give up. Our physical body is becoming older and weaker, but our spirit inside us is made new every day. We have small troubles for a while now, but they are helping us gain an eternal glory that is much greater than the troubles. We set our eyes not on what we see but on what we cannot see. What we see will last only a short time, but what we cannot see will last forever.[2]

The bright glasses of hope help us to focus on eternal things. The dark glasses of despair, on the other hand, lead us to focus on the temporary situations, circumstances, and annoying people right in front of us. Difficulties come in all shapes and sizes. There is no one-size-fits-all. One woman may be struggling with a difficult marriage, another with inadequate finances, another with a rebellious teenager, another with a physical disability. The question is not, what are you going through? The question is, how will you choose to view what you are going through? Hope looks past the circumstances and sees the possibilities!

After I presented the glasses analogy to one group of ladies, a woman came up to me and said, "I'm going straight to Wal-Mart, and I'm going to buy two pairs of glasses, one bright pair and one dark pair. I'm going to put them by my kitchen sink to help me remember that I have a choice every day as to how I will view my world and my circumstances." Not a bad idea!

Prying Our Hands off the Past

Often when we find it difficult to put on the bright glasses of hope, it's because we have our heads turned to the past. We tend to want to hold on to "the good ol' days." Along with the good, though, we also tend to hold on to past hurts, disappointments, and failures. But hope does not live in our pasts. As L. Thomas Holdcroft says, "The past is a guidepost, not a hitching post."[3] Hope looks forward to what God can do in our lives, despite the past.

The apostle Paul had a full and interesting past—some good, some not so good. He was both a Jew and a Roman citizen, schooled under the tutelage of Gamaliel, one of the finest Jewish teachers of his day. He was serious about his service to God and his attention to the Law. At the same time, he assisted in the killing of many of the early Christians, until he became a believer himself. [4] Paul could have taken great pride in his education and Roman citizenship. He also could have wallowed in regret for the way he persecuted believers. Instead of looking back at the past, however, he chose to look forward with hope toward God's plans for his future. He declared,

"Brothers and sisters, I know that I have not yet reached that goal [of being all that God wants me to be], but there is one thing I always do. Forgetting the past and straining toward what is ahead, I keep trying to reach the goal and get the prize for which God called me through Christ to the life above."[5]

Isn't it funny the things we hold on to? Sometimes I'm guilty of holding on to past accomplishments, awards, and successes. Even worse, I'm guilty of holding on to past mistakes and failures, rolling them over and over in my mind. It's easy to rehearse past hurts and bitterness, isn't it? But whether we hold on to bad things or good things, we miss God's plan for us when we focus on the past. We need to pry our hands off the past and turn our sights to what God has ahead for us.

Interestingly, even Jesus spoke about leaving the past behind. As He was walking with His disciples, a man came up to Him and said, "'I will follow you, Lord, but first let me go and say good-bye to my family.' Jesus said, 'Anyone who begins to plow a field but keeps looking back is of no use in the kingdom of God.'"[6] What is Jesus saying to us in this passage? He is calling us to a new level of security—not a security based on the past and what we have always known, but one that is based on our trust in God's faithfulness for the future.

You see, hope isn't based on the past. It isn't based on our present circumstances, either, or on the possibility that things will turn out okay, since we have no guarantee that life will be smooth sailing. Nor is our hope based on people, for they will inevitably let us down (just as we are bound to let others down a time or two). The only sure foundation on which we can build our hope is God Himself. As Edward Mote wrote in his great nineteenth-century hymn of faith, "My hope is built on nothing less than Jesus' blood and righteousness; I dare not trust the sweetest frame, but wholly lean on Jesus' name. On Christ, the solid Rock, I stand; all other ground is sinking sand; all other ground is sinking sand."[7]

How to Build Hope

Yes, the words of that hymn are true, you may be thinking, *but how do I build hope into my life, practically speaking?* Hope comes as we focus our eyes heavenward. When we set our focus on things above, the temporary troubles of this world look smaller and less significant. As we heard Paul say earlier, "We set our eyes not on what we see but on what we cannot see." He reiterated this point in his letter to the Colossians: "Since you have been raised to new life with Christ, set your sights on the realities of heaven, where Christ sits at God's right hand in the place of honor and power. Let heaven fill your thoughts. Do not think only about things down here on earth."[8]

That upward focus becomes clearer as we spend time in God's Word. As we read of God's faithfulness, mercy, and goodness, our hope is increased. When we reflect on Bible story after Bible story of God's great love, power, and forgiveness, our hope is built up and our foundation of trust in Him alone is strengthened.

Take a look at the words of Psalm 42. In this passage, the psalmist chooses to remove the dark glasses of despair and put on the bright glasses of hope:

As a deer thirsts for streams of water,
    so I thirst for you, God.
I thirst for the living God.
    When can I go to meet with him?
Day and night, my tears have been my food.
People are always saying,
    "Where is your God?"
When I remember these things,
    I speak with a broken heart.
I used to walk with the crowd
    and lead them to God's Temple
    with songs of praise.

Why am I so sad?
  Why am I so upset?
I should put my hope in God
  and keep praising him,
  my Savior and my God.
I am very sad . . .
Troubles have come again and again, sounding like waterfalls.
  Your waves are crashing all around me.
The LORD shows his true love every day.
  At night I have a song,
  and I pray to my living God.
I say to God, my Rock,
  "Why have you forgotten me?
Why am I sad
  and troubled by my enemies?"
My enemies' insults make me feel
  as if my bones were broken.
They are always saying,
  "Where is your God?"

Why am I so sad?
  Why am I so upset?
I should put my hope in God
  and keep praising him,
  my Savior and my God.

The psalmist had troubles, just as we all do. He felt sad, lonely, and down. Can you relate? Yet he made a decision to turn from despair to hope, and the conduit was praise. He made a conscious decision to "put my hope in God and keep praising him." Our hope, like the psalmist's, is founded on God. Praising Him encourages us to turn our focus heavenward and reflect, not on our temporary struggles, but on His eternal sovereignty and power.

Take this simple step, as the writer of Psalm 42 did. Start each morning with praise. After you push that snooze button one last time, jump in the shower, get dressed for work, or run to the nursery to pick up a hungry baby, turn your heart heavenward and begin to praise. Say, "Father, I praise You, for You hold the world in Your hands. You have all power and strength and wisdom. I look to You, O High King of Heaven, for my help and hope today."

Put your hope in God, and keep on praising Him! Then throw away those dark glasses. You won't be needing them anymore.

Calming Thoughts

Scripture Reading: Luke 8:22–56, "Four Hopeless-to-Hopeful Situations"

Quiet Meditations:
- Describe the four hopeless situations in this passage.
- How did Jesus bring hope to each one?
- Which person or persons can you relate to: the followers who forgot who was in the boat with them, the man shackled with chains, the sick woman who reached out to touch Jesus, or the desperate man who fell at Jesus' feet?

Personal Prayer:
I praise You, God of all Creation. I praise You for being my Savior, my help, and my hope. I praise You that You are able to handle every situation, for You hold my life in Your hands. I confess that I fail to turn to You at times, and I try to find my hope in other things. But I know that You are my only true hope in time of need. Help me to keep my focus heavenward, to look up to You instead of at my circumstances. Give me Your hope and peace and joy. In Jesus' name I pray, amen.

13

Keeping Your Sanity in the Suffering

Tears are often the telescope by which we see far into heaven.
HENRY WARD BEECHER

The sufferings we have now are nothing compared to the great glory that will be shown to us. Everything God made is waiting with excitement for God to show his children's glory completely.

ROMANS 8:18–19

If I were to ask every mom who reads this book to describe what suffering looks like, I would get millions of different answers. That is, of course, assuming that millions of moms read this book. (Now that's wearing the bright glasses of hope, isn't it?) My point is, suffering differs based on each person's perspective. One mom may be suffering through a challenging pregnancy; another may be suffering through a bankruptcy hearing; another may be suffering because her child has been diagnosed with a severe learning disability, and simply making it through one day of schoolwork is an overwhelming struggle.

Perhaps you could safely say you're not going through any type of suffering at the present time. Or maybe you're in the midst of intense pain at this very moment. Whatever your situation, this chapter is written to bring you to a place of peace, strength, and trust. It may serve as preparation for a possible storm in the future, or it may offer much-needed, welcome words of calm and healing in the midst of a current one. The truth is we all suffer at one time or another. And whether that's our reality now or some time in the future, we can benefit from an exploration of what the Bible has to say about God and the issue of suffering.

Beauty from Ashes

Surprisingly, the Bible is not filled with happy stories about nearly perfect people who lived blissful lives. On the contrary, it's filled with true stories about real people who experienced challenges, pain, disappointments, and loss. Yet the beauty of these stories is that there is victory and redemption in each one. Joseph suffered persecution, slavery, and imprisonment, yet God redeemed his life from the pit and raised him up to a place of honor. The Israelites suffered under Egyptian slavery, yet God freed them from their chains and brought them out of Egypt in a miraculous way. Daniel, Jonah, Samson, Job, and most of the prophets suffered significantly, yet each of them also experienced God's strength, comfort, and deliverance.

Now I'm not suggesting that every difficulty in our lives is going to morph into a bed of roses, or that circumstances will always play out just the way we want them to. But I am saying that God can bring redemption to even the worst of situations. He can heal our broken hearts, give us a new start, and help us experience blessing and spiritual growth *through the suffering*. In the midst of his own suffering, Job knew that God was with him, even though he couldn't see Him. "But God knows the way that I take, and when he has tested me, I will come out like gold," he said. "My feet have closely followed his steps; I have stayed in his way; I did not turn aside."[1]

To consider the greatest suffering of all time, we need look no further than the cross. Christ chose to go to the cross and pay for our sins by suffering and dying on our behalf. And through that suffering, God brought the greatest redemption the earth has ever known. Now if God did not spare His only Son, but allowed Him to suffer on our behalf, then certainly we can expect to suffer at various points in our own lives. The good news is God brought redemption to the whole world through the death of His Son, and He can redeem our suffering too. He may not do it in the way we expect, but we can rest in the knowledge that God is able to take any circumstance and bring good from it.

In Psalm 103, David reflected on the attributes and characteristics of God. He described God as the One "who redeems your life from the pit and crowns you with love and compassion."[2] David understood that God is a God of redemption and hope. In the fire of suffering, we can feel His love and care and trust Him to bring something good out of the ashes. The Bible explains it this way: "For just as the sufferings of Christ flow over into our lives, so also through Christ our comfort overflows."[3]

No Surprise

When suffering happens to us as Christians, we shouldn't be surprised. That was Peter's message to the early Christians: "Dear friends, don't be surprised at the fiery trials you are going through, as if something strange were happening to you. Instead, be very glad— because these trials will make you partners with Christ in his suffering, and afterward you will have the wonderful joy of sharing his glory when it is displayed to all the world."[4]

My friend Jill Scott has experienced a double dose of trials in her life, yet her sufferings have only served to strengthen her faith and love for God. I want you to read her story in her own words:

When my husband and I married in 1995, he already had two children from a previous marriage and I had one. In 1996, we had our first child together and in 1997, our second. We were very happy but very busy with our new blended family. In March of 1999, to my surprise, I found out I was pregnant again. What was God thinking? I truly thought there was no way I could handle another pregnancy or another child.

Immediately I turned to the Lord in prayer and thanked Him for this big surprise and asked Him to take care of our baby and our family. He revealed to me that this child was His, and like all children, He had very special plans for her.

On December 18, 1999, our baby girl, Madison, was born. She was an angel. She hardly cried. She ate and slept well. She was a new mother's dream. The doctor said she was healthy, so we went home from the hospital as scheduled. I remember thinking how awesome God was because He knew we couldn't have handled anything shy of a wonderful baby.

In May of 2000 that dream became a nightmare. Our perfect baby, Madison, became very ill. Her eyes, head, and neck were all locked to one side. I couldn't get her to focus or turn her head. Frantically I rushed her to the pediatrician, and he sent us straight to the hospital. As I drove down the highway I began repeating, "Do not be afraid. Do not be afraid." I prayed and cried out to the Lord for help. I prayed that nothing serious would be wrong with our precious daughter.

After two days of testing, we received the tragic news. Our baby had a very rare, sometimes fatal, metabolic disease. The disease affects approximately one in 30,000 births, and there is no cure. The disease is called GA-1, or Glutaric

Aciduria Type 1. The doctors told us that Madison had received severe brain damage from this disease. They said she would never be normal again.

Devastated and scared, I held Madison close to my chest and cried. A nurse kindly asked if she could call my pastor. We quickly discovered that we went to the same church. I knew that was not a coincidence. There were hundreds of nurses who worked in this hospital, and God had sent the one from my church to remind me of His presence. I knew He was up to something big. I pictured God looking down and selecting our family for this very rare job, and I didn't want to let Him down. As crushed as I was, I decided to trust God and grow instead of doubt God and die inside. With this decision, He began to give me peace in the middle of a terrible storm.

There were many days I felt God had made a big mistake in selecting our family for this huge job, but I was quickly reminded that He makes no mistakes. My friends were there to make sure I didn't forget how much God loved me and that He would never give me more than I could handle. My friend Amy brought praise music to our hospital room and taped scriptures on our walls. The room turned into a small sanctuary. My friends, family, and church were always there for us.

Madison was in a lot of pain. She had lost normal use of her arms, legs, and head. She could no longer roll over or suck her thumb. She vomited frequently and had trouble taking her bottle. I actually pleaded with God to take her to heaven. Well, He didn't. He chose to keep her here on earth and change many lives . . . especially mine.

Madison has taught me more about life and love than I ever dreamed. She has taught me more about God's heart and what He desires for all of us. She has taught me about courage and hope. She has taught me about how special we all are, even if we look and act differently than others.

Madison has changed my life and my heart dramatically. What I first thought was yet another shattered dream was actually a blessing in disguise. Yes, my life is much more challenging, but it is far more rewarding. Madison is now almost five years old. She still cannot walk, talk, or eat properly. She has a feeding tube in her stomach and thirteen weekly therapy sessions. She also has a beautiful smile, a fun personality, and magical eyes with which she can communicate. She is perfect—perfect in God's eyes.

Since the onset of Madison's illness, God has continued to allow other major trials in my life, and I know there are more to come. With each one I apply the rule of Madison's disease: GA-1. Medically, the acronym stands for Glutaric Aciduria Type 1, but I use it to handle all the circumstances in my life. For me, it stands for God Always First.[5]

Survival Tips for Suffering

Maybe you are in the midst of some kind of suffering, and you want to make the best of it. Like Jill, you want to "trust God and grow instead of doubt God and die inside." How do you survive and keep your sanity? How do you practice "God Always First" in the midst of your struggle? Here are three simple words that can help: *know*, *grow*, and *go*. Let's look at each one individually.

Know That God Is with You

Know that God is with you through the suffering. He has not left you. He loves you. You are His precious child. In the Old Testament, God spoke to the Israelites through His prophets. Isaiah gave them the following message, which still speaks to us today:

Now this is what the LORD says.
   He created you, people of Jacob;
   he formed you, people of Israel.
He says, "Don't be afraid, because I have saved you.
   I have called you by name, and you are mine.
When you pass through the waters, I will be with you.
   When you cross rivers, you will not drown.
When you walk through fire, you will not be burned,
   nor will the flames hurt you.
This is because I, the LORD, am your God,
   the Holy One of Israel, your Savior."[6]

There is no greater comfort than knowing that God is with us. He reminds us of this fact over and over in Scripture. As Jesus departed this earth, He said, "I will be with you always, even until the end of this age."[7] Often God's loving presence is made known to us through the Holy Spirit, whom He has given to comfort and strengthen us; other times it is felt through the flesh-and-blood people He provides to help us in our time of need. Even Jesus, in His hour of need in the Garden of Gethsemane, asked His disciples to stay close by. He wanted their companionship and their prayers.

Godly friends can be God's gift to you during suffering. Know that God is with you, and know that He will provide the people you need to encourage you and help you through your ordeal. Receive His help through the hands of faith-filled friends.

Use Suffering as an Opportunity to Grow

Look at suffering as an opportunity to *grow*—in spiritual maturity, in character, in wisdom, and in experience. James reminds us, "Dear brothers and sisters, whenever trouble comes your way, let it be an opportunity for joy. For when your faith is tested, your endurance has a chance to grow. So let it grow, for when your endurance is fully developed, you will be strong in character and ready for anything."[8]

The first step toward growth is acceptance. In the Old Testament, Job didn't understand why God had allowed his suffering, but he still accepted it. His wife told him to curse God and die, but Job responded, "Shall we indeed accept good from God and not accept adversity?"[9] Accepting adversity doesn't mean embracing it and loving it, but rather realizing that God has allowed it in our lives. Our growth continues as we look to God in humble expectation of what He can do through the situation.

Ultimately we grow not by our own strength, but in His strength. "Be strong in the Lord and in the power of His might,"[10] Paul wrote to the Ephesians. Fall into His arms and allow Him to help you through the ordeal. In Romans we read, "So what should we say about this? If God is with us, no one can defeat us. He did not spare his own Son but gave him for us all. So with Jesus, God will surely give us all things."[11] God can be trusted to give you what you need for your journey of growth.

Go Out and Help Others

Use your experience with suffering as an opportunity to *go* and help other people who are hurting. Giving consolation to others is a tender healer of our own souls. When we help others, we take our eyes off our own pain and put them on something more constructive. "Praise be to the God and Father of our Lord Jesus Christ," Paul wrote to the early Christians, who certainly faced their own share of struggles. "God is the Father who is full of mercy and all comfort. He comforts us every time we have trouble, so when others have trouble, we can comfort them with the same comfort God gives us."[12]

You don't necessarily have to go looking for opportunities to minister—although, if God compels you to seek out others who are hurting, do so. Just be watchful and open as God brings those who are struggling to your doorstep. You may want to consider starting a small support group in your community. That's what author and Women of Faith speaker Barbara Johnson did. Because of the pain she experienced in her own life, she started Spatula Ministries, a support group for parents who have suffered heartache or loss. Over many years, thousands of parents have been helped by her ministry. Don't feel overwhelmed by her example, though. You don't have to minister to thousands—just the ones God brings into your life.

So how do you keep your sanity in the midst of suffering? Know, grow, and go. Know that God is with you and will never leave you. Know that He will provide friends and other people who will help you through your ordeal. Grow in His strength, accepting what you cannot change and expecting what only He can do. Go to others who are suffering in similar situations and give them a loving word or an encouraging embrace, thereby helping yourself to heal in the process.

I want to close this chapter with a little poem. May it encourage each of us to turn our eyes off our struggles and onto our great God. Only then will we experience true calm and peace, even in the midst of suffering:

> God hath not promised
> Skies always blue,
> Flower-strewn pathways
> All our lives through.
> God hath not promised
> Sun without rain,
> Joy without sorrow,
> Peace without pain.
> God hath not promised
> We shall not know
> Toil and temptation,
> Trouble and woe.
> He hath not told us
> We shall not bear
> Many a burden,
> Many a care.

But God hath promised
Strength for the day,
Rest for the laborer,
Light for the way,
Grace for the trials,
Help from above,
Unfailing sympathy,
Undying love.[13]

Calming Thoughts

Scripture Reading: John 16, "Jesus Prepares His Followers"

Quite Meditations:
- What kind of word picture did Jesus paint for His disciples in describing the days ahead?
- What comfort did He give them?
- Which verses in this passage are particularly meaningful to you personally?

Personal Prayer:
God of peace and comfort, I praise You for Your undying love toward me. You never leave me or forsake me. I praise You because You know all things and can do all things. I confess that it's hard for me to accept suffering. I am weak, but You are strong. Help me and hold me through the pain. I look to You for comfort and peace. Give me strength each day to do what I need to do, and give me the support I need through Your Holy Spirit and the people You send my way. Thank You for being my rock and my refuge, a very present help in time of need. In Jesus' name I pray, amen.

step
five

Strengthen Family Relationships

Family life is too intimate to be preserved by the spirit of justice. It can be sustained by a spirit of love which goes beyond justice.

REINHOLD NIEBUHR

How wonderful it is, how pleasant,
when brothers live together in harmony!

PSALM 133:1 NLT

When there is peace and understanding between family members, tension is relieved, stress is diminished, and calm prevails. Relationships take work; but as they are strengthened, joy permeates the home.

14

Are You Enjoying or Annoying Your Family?

Bringing up a family should be an adventure,
not an anxious discipline in which everybody is
constantly graded for performance.

MILTON R. SAPIRSTEIN

Children are a gift from the LORD;
they are a reward from him.

PSALM 127:3 NLT

My education prepared me for practical things in life, such as how to find the square root of 256 or write an eight-page report on Rio de Janeiro. But I don't remember any classes preparing me for the challenges I would face in the biggest job of all: parenting. In her book *Just Wait Till You Have Children of Your Own*, Erma Bombeck shares her perspective on "parental education":

"Why don't you grow up?"

If I said it to them once, I said it a million times. Is it my imagination or have I spent a lifetime shutting refrigerator doors, emptying nose tissue from pants pockets before washing, writing checks for milk, picking up wet towels, and finding library books in the clothes hamper?

Mr. Matterling said, "Parenting is loving." (What did he know? He was my old Child Psychology teacher who didn't have any children. He only had twenty-two guppies and two catfish to clean the bowl.) How I wish that for one day I could teach Mr. Matterling's class. How I would like to tell him it's more than loving. More than cleaning gravel. More than eating the ones you don't like.

Parenting is frustration that you have to see to believe. Would I ever have imagined there would be whole days when I didn't have time to comb my hair? Mornings after a slumber party when I looked like Margaret Mead with a migraine? Could I have ever comprehended that something so simple, so beautiful, and so uncomplicated as a child could drive you to shout, "We are a family and you're part of this family and . . . you're going to spend a Friday night with us having a good time if we have to chain you to the bed!"[1]

Yes, parenting encompasses much more than love. It also holds in its arms fear, anger, joy, disappointment, sorrow, and splendor. There is no easy way to describe our job as mothers, much less prepare. But one thing we know beyond a shadow of a doubt: While parenting is more than love, love is absolutely essential. As moms we all want to raise our kids in a loving manner.

A Bother or a Blessing?

Recently after I spoke to a group of young moms, the women asked me to stay for a question and answer session. Now Q and As are always a little scary for me. Despite the fact that I've written a few books on parenting, I readily admit I don't have all the answers.

During Q and A times, I have to rely on God's wisdom to see me through. If I don't know an answer, I humbly say so.

That particular day a lady asked, "How do you maintain a good relationship with your kids in the midst of disciplining them and training them, so that when they grow up they won't resent you?"

Here's how I answered (by God's grace): "While our children are young, we must discipline with love and understanding. We must be consistent and fair. If we scream and yell and our kids feel misunderstood, then resentment will build up over the years. Listen to your children; study them. Don't just discipline the surface issues; get to the heart and let your children know you really care about them. Enjoy your kids rather than being continually annoyed by them. If you enjoy them, they will pick up on your heartfelt sincerity, your tender love, and your consistent discipline. If you feel as if they're a constant bother, they'll pick up on that too."

The essence of that answer became the foundation of this chapter. Certainly our end goal is not to be loved and appreciated by our children. Our goal is to raise godly, confident, well-balanced kids—with the natural end result being strong, loving, and enjoyable relationships with them as they become young adults. Our hope is that others will be able to say of us what Solomon said about Mrs. Proverbs 31: "Her children rise up and call her blessed."[2]

Be honest now: Do you see your kids as small harassing creatures sent to bug you, or do you see them as blessings from God? The answer to that question may depend on what kind of day you're having! All kidding aside, it is interesting to see how much our perspective changes after those first beautiful days of bliss, when we hold our precious bundles of joy in our arms for the first time. Somehow, between more years, more kids, more diapers, and more laundry, the bliss seemed to go out the window.

Deep down inside we don't want to be annoying to our kids, and we don't want to be annoyed by them. We want to enjoy them, and we want them to enjoy us. The question, practically speaking, is how? What is the key to enjoying our children and strengthening our relationships with them?

In this chapter we're going to answer that question from two angles. The first has to do with our learning how *not* to be annoying to our families. We'll discover ways to avoid being nit-picky with our kids, for example. The second angle has to do with our learning how to truly enjoy our children. They really are gifts from God, and we need to see them as such. In this section we'll learn how to start moving *away* from annoying and *toward* enjoying.

Destroying Our Tendency to Be Annoying

Three words should be in every mom's personal parenting handbook: *consistency*, *communication*, and *confidence*. These three words won't make us perfect parents, but they will assist us in destroying some of our most annoying tendencies as moms and help us find the balance between ineffective discipline and obnoxious overkill. That beautiful balance is the key to bringing up children who become healthy, well-balanced adults.

The Importance of Consistency

When it comes to discipline, consistency is difficult to work out on a daily basis. It demands both wisdom and attention. Still, it's well worth pursuing, since haphazard discipline tends to breed disrespect in our kids. Of course, it's impossible to be perfectly consistent; with children, situations will always arise that call for personalized rather than fixed responses. But as often as possible, we need to practice consistency without being rigid. We need to give our kids the assurance that consistency is a priority for us.

Our kids are watching our example. That means that when we say we're going to do something, we should do it. When we say we believe that going to church is important, we should go regularly. When we say that gossip is wrong, we should guard our mouths.

When we say a certain consequence will follow if our kids disobey, then we must carry through with it.

My own mother was a beautiful example of consistency. She told my sister and me that it was important to be kind to others, both in actions and in words. She taught us to never gossip or say unkind things about people behind their backs. If we ever did, she let us know we were in the wrong. Ultimately, however, we learned more about kindness from her example than from her discipline. She not only taught us to speak kindly about others; she did so herself. I never once heard her gossip or put someone down.

More than anything else, young people need to see authenticity in adults. They need to see parents who consistently walk their talk. Our kids will find us less annoying if they can trust our words—if they can be confident that (1) our discipline is fair and consistent, and (2) we're living our own lives by the principles we're teaching them.

Effective Communication

As a general rule, we need to focus our attention on encouraging our children in what they are doing right, rather than spending all our time correcting them for every little thing they do wrong. We need to be encouragers who give them strength with our words, rather than discouragers who continually get on their case with our words.

Certainly there is a time for discipline and training, but even our punishment should be handled with positive communication. As we punish, we must make sure that our children understand why they are being punished and what they should have done instead (that is, what the correct behavior would have been in that situation). As often as possible, we need to provide an answer to that dreaded question, "Why do I have to . . . ?" Sometimes we're tempted to respond, "Because I said so," but that's really not helpful. We need to try to communicate at least a simple explanation, so that our children will accept their punishment with less resentment.

We also need to be willing to hear their objections—if they present them respectfully. We shouldn't be too quick to say, "I don't want to hear it." A better approach would be to ask, "Do you want to talk about this? I really want to understand what is bothering you." Taking this track doesn't mean we're obliged to change our minds about an appropriate punishment; it simply demonstrates our willingness to build a better understanding between us and our children.

Developing Confidence

When I say confidence, I don't mean our own self-confidence. I am referring to the confidence we have in the Lord and His ability to care for our kids. The most annoying moms are the ones that hover over their children, trying to prevent every little cut or scrape, every minor rejection or pain. As our children grow up, we must wisely and carefully step back and stop trying to protect them from every hurt or disappointment in life. We must allow them to fall and scrape their knees, to feel the pain of losing sometimes, to bear the natural consequences of their actions and learn from their mistakes.

The truth is our children's greatest learning opportunities often come from their failures and disappointments. We must have the God-confidence to believe they will grow from both the good and the bad experiences of life. Henry Ward Beecher put it this way: "The true idea of self-restraint is to let a child venture . . . The mistakes of children are often better than their no-mistakes."[3] Certainly we do not hope for failure and disappointment for our kids. But a greater enemy than failure and disappointment is a mom who shields her child from every conceivable hurt. Children who are overprotected when they are young grow up to be adults who have no idea how to cope with negative situations.

How to Enjoy Motherhood

Enjoying our families can be one of life's richest rewards for us as moms. But unless we're deliberate in choosing and embracing that enjoyment, the cares of this life are likely to choke the joy away. The choice is like a coin with two sides. We must choose to take joy in our families—which means choosing to be less annoyed by individual family members. Easier said than done, right? Allow me to share a simple plan to encourage more enjoyment and less annoyance in your home. Just remember these three words: *stop*, *look*, and *listen*.

First, *stop* expecting your family members to be just like you. Each person in your family was created by God to be unique and special. If you have ever studied personality traits, you know that some personalities are naturally driven to succeed; others love to have fun; others are worker bees behind the scenes; and still others are easygoing, without a care in the world. Most of us are a combination or blend of two or more personality traits.

The problem arises when we don't understand that our sons or daughters (or spouses, for that matter) are different from us. They're bound to react differently to situations and feel differently when circumstances change. We begin to experience true enjoyment, however, when we stop being annoyed by these differences and begin to appreciate each person's uniqueness. God made us different for a purpose. Let's rejoice in the differences and appreciate the fact that God intentionally blends different people together to form unique families—each one collectively beautiful in God's sight.

Second, *look* for the good qualities in each of your children (and your spouse too). Focus on their strengths, not just their weaknesses. Imagine an invisible sign on each person's chest that reads, "I want to feel important." Make it your job to help them feel that way! Build up your family members and help them see their own good character qualities. Thank the Lord for the gift those qualities are to you.

As you do these things, you're bound to find that you're enjoying your family immensely. Why? Because you are seeing them as a treasure, and you are blessing them in the process. There is great joy in helping others be the best they can be—especially when they live under the same roof with us.

Finally, *listen* to your family members. Get to know them by really listening when they share about what makes them happy, as well as when they share their frustrations and anger. Study your children by truly hearing them. Be attentive to their hearts as you listen for the message that's below the surface level of words.

Your teenage daughter, for example, may lash out at you for not being allowed to go to a certain party; but if you really listen, you may hear the sound of an underlying loneliness in her heart. You can respond, then, not to her harsh words, but to her heart's cry, helping her to understand that going to the party will not bring her the good, long-term friendships she seeks. You can also offer positive suggestions for developing new friendships. The result: She still can't go to the party, but now she feels heard and understood, and she can begin to move in a positive direction toward alleviating her sense of loneliness.

When we demand a behavior without giving our children an opportunity to feel heard or understood, we open the doors to defiance and rebellion—and annoyance. Stopping, looking, and listening, however, lead to enjoyment of our families and of each family member individually. Why? Because joy develops when we appreciate, encourage, and understand one another. Let's start enjoying, not annoying! The following verses by A. F. Bayley can be our prayer:

Help us, O Lord, our homes to make
Thy Holy Spirit's dwelling place;
Our hands and hearts' devotion take
To be the servants of thy grace.[4]

Calming Thoughts

Scripture Reading: Colossians 3, "What Christians Should Do"

Quiet Meditations:
- What do you learn about relating to others in this passage?
- What behaviors are we told to get rid of in our lives?
- How can you apply the truths in this passage to your family life?

Personal Prayer:
Glorious Father, You are so good to me. I'm so thankful for the great and mighty work You are doing in my life and in the life of my family. I praise You for the joy that You give. Thank You for each family member. Thank You for their wonderful, easy-to-love qualities, and thank You for their more challenging qualities. I'm glad You made each one of us unique and special. I confess that sometimes I focus on the annoying qualities of my family members instead of on the beautiful ones. Help me to stop, look, listen, and enjoy the tremendous family You have given to me. In Jesus' name I pray, amen.

Sacred Secrets to Staying Connected

Family is even more important today than in generations past, and its erosion is unacceptable . . .

As a parent you have the power to set your child on a course for success.

You may or may not feel powerful right now, but if you have the courage to rise to the challenge, your child can and will be blessed beyond belief.

DR. PHIL MCGRAW

Your love must be real. Hate what is evil, and hold on to what is good. Love each other like brothers and sisters.
Give each other more honor than you want for yourselves.

ROMANS 12:9–10

We really do need each other. In a society that celebrates independence and self-sufficiency, we tend to brush aside the truth that we need person-to-person intimacy and connection. In generations past, family was the place people found their connection and acceptance. Now due to the busyness of life and the breakdown of the family, many teenagers and young adults find themselves search-ing for intimacy in other places—drugs, gangs, sex, cults, and alco-hol, to name a few.

Strengthening the bonds between family members can't solve all of society's problems. But stronger family connections can certainly help dissuade young people from searching elsewhere for intimacy. And while the best time to start building those bonds is when our kids are young, it's never too late to begin applying the sacred secrets to staying connected.

Why do I call them "sacred secrets"? Because they're long-established principles about family ties found in God's sacred Word. Are they secrets? Not really, except in the sense that they're not talked about much in today's society. Most modern families don't think to look to the Bible for guidance and direction. My hope is that as we bring four of these sacred, time-honored "secrets" to the surface, we will see a revival of family connectedness in our culture. It *can* happen—one home at a time.

You see, the sacred secrets of staying connected are simple, yet powerful. How do I know they're powerful? Because I didn't make them up; God did! I'm simply gleaning them from God's Word. If you want to build intimacy and connectedness within your family, the Bible encourages you to

1. Strengthen the bond between you and your spouse.
2. Express genuine love.
3. Give from the heart.
4. Meet your family members where they are.

Perhaps you're thinking, *I'm not sure I recognize these four points from Scripture.* Trust me, they're there. Follow with me as we discover the wonderful family secrets purposely nestled in God's sacred Word.

1. Strengthen the Bond
between You and Your Spouse

The bond between a husband and a wife is a powerful influence in keeping a family connected, intimate, and strong. That's because God's plan for families is established on the foundation of a man and a woman. We read in Genesis:

> And the LORD God said, "It is not good for the man to be alone. I will make a companion who will help him" . . . So the LORD God caused Adam to fall into a deep sleep. He took one of Adam's ribs and closed up the place from which he had taken it. Then the LORD God made a woman from the rib and brought her to Adam.
>
> "At last!" Adam exclaimed. "She is part of my own flesh and bone! She will be called 'woman,' because she was taken out of a man." This explains why a man leaves his father and mother and is joined to his wife, and the two are united into one.[1]

When I think of examples of connected families, I think of my dear friend Amy. I asked her to share some of her thoughts on how her family has been able to stay connected over the years. She naturally started with her relationship with her husband, Mike. Here's how she put it:

> Mike and I have a commitment to stay connected as husband and wife. We feel that if our relationship suffers, then our family will suffer. We try to get away a couple of times each year, just the two of us. We view this as a priority. Yes, there are hassles involved in getting all the details of the kids' schedules worked out, but it is so worth it in the long run!
>
> Getting away doesn't have to be a two-week vacation to the Greek isles; it can be a weekend at a bed-and-breakfast or

even camping out for a couple of nights. These little retreats have given us the time we need to unwind with each other, reconnect, and revive the intimacy that can so easily get lost in the hustle-bustle of everyday living in the twenty-first century.[2]

Strengthening the bond between husband and wife takes work, but the portrait that it paints for the family is beautiful. The apostle Paul encouraged the bond of marriage using the most glorious of illustrations: "As the Scriptures say, 'A man leaves his father and mother and is joined to his wife, and the two are united into one.' This is a great mystery, but it is an illustration of the way Christ and the church are one. So again I say, each man must love his wife as he loves himself, and the wife must respect her husband."[3]

Perhaps you have experienced divorce in your family or the death of your spouse. Don't be discouraged and think that this sacred secret doesn't apply to you. If you are divorced, I encourage you, if at all possible, to maintain a good, strong relationship with your ex. Be civil with him. Don't tear him down with your words. Do what you can together to provide a united front in raising your kids. I realize this may be impossible in certain situations; just do the best you can with God's help.

Whether you are widowed or divorced, ask the Lord to bring a father figure into your kids' lives. And above all, remember that the ultimate father is God Himself. King David recognized this when he wrote, "If my father and mother leave me, the LORD will take me in."[4] The Lord can certainly take over where absent or imperfect parents have left off.

2. Express Genuine Love

I'm sure all of us say we love our families, but how does that play out in our actions? Paul told his fellow Christians, "Your love must be real."[5] The apostle John explained further: "My children, we should love people not only with words and talk, but by our actions and true caring."[6] Our love both inside and outside our homes must go beyond words. It must be seen, not just heard. This kind of real, demonstrated love is not a love that comes naturally to us, however. Oh sure, we talk about a "mother's love" as if it's a nearly angelic type of love; but the truth is, perfect love comes from God alone. Only His love is real, sincere, and true.

John went on to talk about love this way:

Dear friends, we should love each other, because love comes from God. Everyone who loves has become God's child and knows God. Whoever does not love does not know God, because God is love. This is how God showed his love to us: He sent his one and only Son into the world so that we could have life through him. This is what real love is: It is not our love for God; it is God's love for us in sending his Son to be the way to take away our sins.[7]

God connected with mankind through the ultimate demonstration of love, by sacrificially sending His Son into this world. If we want to begin to know and show real love to our families, we must first know God's love and allow it to flow from us. As we recognize and delight in His love for us, we are enabled and empowered to show it to others. Genuine love is above all a selfless love. Here are a few characteristics:

- A kind and gentle tone of voice
- Sacrificial patience
- Loving discipline
- Forgiving an affront (after proper discipline)
- Sincere listening
- Serving one another
- A hug, a touch, a smile
- Eye contact

Ask God to show you how you can best demonstrate love to each of your family members. People receive love in different ways, so it's important to know what makes your family members feel loved and then learn to express your love to each one in a unique way. My daughter Grace, for example, feels loved when I give her little unexpected gifts. My daughter Joy feels loved when we spend quality time together. My husband, Curt, receives love through acts of service I do for him. Personally, I receive love best through words of affirmation. We have four people in our house—and four different ways we give and receive love![8]

As moms, we need to especially encourage two areas of family love and bonding: loving-kindness between siblings and connection with extended family. The first area has been a particular struggle for me. My two daughters are one year apart in school. As you might expect, it has been natural for them to compare themselves with one another, even though I have tried my hardest to discourage it. Pride, inferiority, and jealousy come into play whenever siblings compare and compete with one another. Believe me, I know!

Of course, sibling rivalry is nothing new. In the Old Testament, we see it take place between the very first siblings, Cain and Abel; between Jacob and Esau; and between Joseph and his eleven brothers. But with God's help, we can make a difference in our own families and encourage our kids to bond in a positive, loving way with one another. How? Here are a few tips I've picked up from my own experience:

- Require them to apologize to one another after disputes.
- Encourage them to go to each other's events and games.
- Allow them to pray together as they say good-night.
- Encourage good discussions at the dinner table.
- Help them see the best in one another.
- Encourage them to be patient with one another and overlook annoyances.

The second area of family connection we need to encourage is bonding with extended family members. This type of bonding begins with our own attitudes. We need to show our kids by example that we recognize the value of extended family and appreciate our family heritage. In my own family, we are blessed to have some of our extended family members living nearby. We all support each other and get together on a regular basis. Knowing that their grandparents are close by and watchful of their actions has built an additional level of accountability in my girls.

Does your extended family live far away? Stay close through e-mail, letters, phone calls, and visits. Do you have past hurts from family struggles that still linger? As much as possible, work past those pains, moving forward in forgiveness for the sake of your children. We need to remember that one day *we* will be the extended family, and our grown kids will take their cues from the example we set for them when they were young.

3. Give from the Heart

Often we hear of doting grandparents or divorced spouses over-indulging children with gifts, thinking that this will win their love. Interestingly, kids tend to see right through material gifts of this nature. What children really want to know is, is there love behind the gift? Gifts can come in all forms and fashions. Some of the best gifts of love are not material at all: for example, the gift of time, a smile, a listening ear, an unexpected blessing, a soothing word, a kind gesture, or a token of thoughtfulness.

Reflect with me for a moment on the Old Testament story of Hannah and her young son, Samuel. As you may recall, Hannah prayed for a son and promised she would dedicate him back to the Lord if she received an answer to her prayer. God granted her request, and she in turn brought young Samuel to live with Eli the priest. Hannah was only able to see her son once a year on her annual visit to the temple in Jerusalem. Still, she found a special way of staying connected.

Scripture tells us that Hannah brought Samuel a homemade coat each year when she came to visit him.[9] A gift from the heart indeed! Can't you just imagine Samuel tenderly holding that coat to his cheek, sniffing it, and running his hands over it? His dear mother had made the coat especially for him! I can picture him wearing it with dignity and pride. It was their family connection. Although they were not close in proximity, they were close in their hearts.

In a similar way, we can give from our hearts to build connectedness with our family members. What might that look like for you? Perhaps it's bringing a lunch to your daughter's school and enjoying a lunchtime visit with your daughter and her friends. Maybe it's a smile and a hug every time your son walks in the door after a long school day. Maybe it's a little something special you picked up at the store for your children because it just made you think of them.

What if you're in a situation that forces you to be away from your children for a length of time due to work, school, divorce, or the simple fact that they are grown and have settled in a different area? You can still remain connected. How? Send a thoughtful e-mail or a handwritten note. Have dinner delivered to them. Pick up and mail a small "I'm just thinking of you" gift. Make a homemade gift and send it. Send pictures. Pick up the phone and offer a listening ear. Use your imagination!

Giving from the heart breeds connectedness. Jesus spoke of giving from the heart and the benefits that result when He said, "If you give, you will receive. Your gift will return to you in full measure, pressed down, shaken together to make room for more, and running over. Whatever measure you use in giving—large or small—it will be used to measure what is given back to you."[10] Now you may have heard this passage used at a church service or on a Christian television program in a message about giving money. But when we read these verses in context, we see that Jesus wasn't talking about giving money; He was talking about giving love, kindness, and for-giveness.

Let's give to our families from the heart. As a natural conse-quence, we will receive in the same manner in which we give. By giv-ing genuine love, we will receive the blessing of connection with our family members. To borrow and twist a phrase from a former presi-dent, "Ask not what your family can do for you; ask what you can do for your family."

4. Meet Your Family Members Where They Are

Possibly one of the most important thoughts we can keep in the fore-front of our minds is that each of our children is a work in progress. As long as they are under our roofs, it's our job to continue to gen-tly teach, train, and discipline them. They're not adults yet, and they aren't finished and complete. Come to think of it, we *are* adults, and we aren't finished either! We all have so much left to learn. None of us are where we ought to be yet.

Growing up is a process. We can't expect our children to be spir-itual giants at the age of eight. They are still developing. We must not berate them for making a mistake in judgment. They are still learn-ing. We cannot give up on them if they are in a stage of rebellion. God is not finished with them yet. Discipline, yes. Punish when nec-essary, yes. But with calm resolve, we need to focus on helping each child learn and grow step by step.

I remember a woman trying to teach me to play the piano when I was seven years old. I just couldn't seem to get it, and she was frustrated with me. At one point she became so exasperated that she cried, "Forget it! You're never going to learn to play the piano!" You can imagine how dejected and discouraged I felt! If only she had chosen to be patient with me, to gently work with my young hands and moldable spirit. Certainly I was not destined to become a concert pianist, but I could have learned to play a few tunes. Instead I became disheartened and gave up.

As moms we have the opportunity to meet our kids where they are each day and gently guide them toward maturity one step at a time. A verse I claim quite often for my family members (and for myself) is Philippians 1:6: "God began doing a good work in you, and I am sure he will continue it until it is finished when Jesus Christ comes again." Our children need us to encourage them in the growth process and not get disgusted with them when they mess up. We must never give them the impression that we are giving up on them. That will only make it more likely that they will give up on themselves.

Meeting our kids where they are doesn't mean we compromise our values. Rather, it means that as we hold our children to proper standards of discipline, we also connect with them through understanding. Certainly this is the type of love and concern God has for us. The Bible tells us that "the Lord disciplines those he loves, and he punishes everyone he accepts as his child."[11] It also says, "The LORD is like a father to his children, tender and compassionate to those who fear him. For he understands how weak we are; he knows we are only dust."[12]

The prophet Isaiah used the illustration of a potter and clay. God is a potter, molding us and making us to be what He created us to be. He is not finished with us yet. I like Isaiah's prayer: "And yet, LORD, you are our Father. We are the clay, and you are the potter. We are all formed by your hand. Oh, don't be so angry with us, LORD. Please don't remember our sins forever. Look at us, we pray, and see that we are all your people."[13] As moms, we need to think of our children relating to us in a similar way. We must gently form them and mold them through loving discipline and understanding, not pound and destroy them in anger and frustration.

The Nitty-Gritty

Do you want the nitty-gritty on how to make these sacred secrets of family connectedness flourish in your home? Here are eight practical suggestions that "put feet on" much of what we've said in this chapter:

Be There for Significant Events

Do everything you can to be at each of your children's per-formances, games, and recitals. After each event, hug them, look them in the eyes, and give them sincere compliments and words of encouragement. If you need to teach them in any way, sandwich the teaching between sincere and specific accolades.

Discipline with Love

The end goal of discipline is to change your children's negative behavior. With that in mind, remember that screaming is an ineffective method for bringing about change. Heart-to-heart communication, on the other hand, combined with wise punishment, will help guide them in the right direction. Always come back together once the punishment is complete, to reassure your children of your love.

Ask Forgiveness When Necessary.

As parents, none of us are perfect. When you make an error or do something wrong, admit it. Apologize. Your children will learn about mistakes, love, forgiveness, and how to apologize through your example. Playing the "I'm a Perfect Person" game only exacerbates family disconnection.

Get to Know Your Children's Friends

One of the best ways to stay connected to your kids is to get to know their friends. Extend a loving hand to their friends and make them feel welcome in your home. Show hospitality. Make your home a good, "clean fun" place to be.

Guard Family Dinnertime with a Passion

Do everything you can to make sure the whole family sits down face to face for dinner several times a week. In today's active society, family dinners are a dying art. Sports practices, music lessons, school meetings, church activities, neighborhood get-togethers, and community projects are all good things in and of themselves, but don't let them rob your family of lively discussions and loving fellowship around the dinner table. My friend Amy makes at least one night a week off-limits to outside activities, so her family can be at home together the entire evening. What a great idea!

Enjoy Family Vacations

Make the time and effort to experience life as a family, away from the normal routine, by enjoying occasional family vacations. Money doesn't have to be an issue. You can go camping, stay at a local motel, visit extended family, or look for travel specials. My fondest memories from my own childhood are of the vacations we took as a family. That's where we really bonded and grew to know and understand one another. Now that I'm a mom, I'm trying to make those same kinds of memories for my own children.

Engage in Meaningful Conversation

Without a doubt, communication is a key connector in family relationships. We will discuss ways to wire your family for communication in the next chapter.

Pray Together

This final nitty-gritty suggestion should come as no surprise. No doubt you've heard it said, "The family that prays together, stays together." I can tell you from experience, it's true. Are you joining together spiritually as a family? I'm not talking about mumbling a quick prayer before you dig into supper. I'm talking about caring enough about each other to pray for each other and encourage one another with the truths of Scripture.

Our spiritual bond in Christ is the greatest connector of all, for family and for all relationships. As we close this chapter, I want us to ponder these words from the apostle Paul: "Be humble and gentle. Be patient with each other, making allowance for each other's faults

175

because of your love. Always keep yourselves united in the Holy Spirit, and bind yourselves together with peace."[14] Let's agree to make this passage a reality in our homes. There is no higher, more sacred secret to staying connected.

Calming Thoughts

Scripture Reading: 1 Corinthians 13, "Love, the Greatest Gift"

Quiet Meditations:
- What do you learn about the importance of love and connection in this passage?
- What are some of the characteristics of love listed here?
- Are you willing to ask God to help you love your family with this kind of love?

Personal Prayer:

God of love, I praise You for loving me so completely. Thank You for showing me genuine love by sending Your Son, Jesus, to die on the cross for my sins. You have truly demonstrated giving from the heart! I confess I need Your help in connecting with my family. Help me to have eyes to see and ears to hear and a heart to understand my family members. May Your Holy Spirit bring us together in the unique way that will work best for us. Thank You for creating our family just the way it is, and help us to honor You together. In Jesus' name I pray, amen.

16

Wiring Your Home
for Family Communication

*There may be no single thing more important in our efforts
to achieve meaningful work and fulfilling relationships
than to learn to practice the art of communication.*

MAX DE PREE

*When you talk, do not say harmful things, but say what
people need—words that will help others become stronger.
Then what you say will do good to those who listen to you.*

EPHESIANS 4:29

The cable guy just left our home moments ago. Ironic, isn't it? Here I am, writing a chapter on wiring our homes for family communication, and a cable guy has just been here to check the wiring in my house. Do you know what he told me? He said we had the wrong wiring! Much to my dismay, he explained that in order to receive digital cable service, we would need to have the entire home rewired with an up-to-date cable system.

Apparently, proper wiring is essential for digital cable communication. Proper wiring is essential for good communication in a family as well. What do I mean by proper family wiring? I'm talking about effective channels of relating that enhance and increase the

177

communication between the people in our households. If your home is like mine, the fast lane of life tends to cause us to bypass those channels, resulting in very little regular, consistent, relationship-building communication. With proper wiring, however, our conversations are enriched, deepening our understanding of one another.

Sometimes old wiring is just fine. Other times it's faulty. Some of us grew up in homes where discussions were vibrant and enjoyable. Family members built each other up and were a positive influence on one another. Others grew up in homes where everyone was consistently negative or sarcastic, and discussions were painful or destructive. Still others grew up in homes where there was very little communication at all, because the television was always on or no one cared to talk with each other.

Whatever kind of home you grew up in, you can wire your current home in a way that facilitates effective family communication. Of course, you may need to change some communication patterns and do a little rewiring, but every family can learn to communicate in ways that are uplifting and meaningful. With the right wiring, we can learn to have conversations that express love, grace, and acceptance to one another. The result? More calm and less stress, of course!

Don't Waste Your Breath

Communication expert Albert Mehrabian says that 55 percent of any message we convey to others is likely to be communicated nonverbally through our actions. Another 38 percent is communicated through our tone of voice. That means only 7 percent of our message is actually communicated through spoken words![1]

Those statistics lead us to the first point we must understand if we want to have effective family communication: Words aren't all that important. Don't get me wrong; we need to choose our words wisely. But if we want our words to be received, we must sandwich them between loving actions and deliver them in tones of kindness.

I know of one family in which the husband rudely demands that his children sit down and have devotions together every evening. (He demands compliance in other areas, too, without offering any understanding or encouragement.) As you can imagine, devotional time in that household is a rather unpleasant experience, and the message often falls on deaf ears.

Certainly it's reasonable to require family members to participate in certain activities (such as family devotions or going to church on Sundays). But instead of being rude and demanding, we can express those requirements in a kind and gentle way that builds, rather than hinders, communication. When our children know that we care enough to listen to them and understand them, even if we don't give in to them, they are more apt to listen and understand the messages we send. Our tone, body language, actions, and lifestyle are the light switches that open up the flow of family communication.

One quick side note: Kindness and gentleness on our part are not an excuse for disrespect from our kids. One teenage girl I know walks all over her overly kind, gentle mother. They don't have healthy communication, because the mother allows the daughter to continually disrespect her. When the mother tries to tell her daughter something, for example, the girl immediately snarls back in a cruel and disrespectful tone.

There is a difference between kindness and foolishness! A wise mom kindly commands respect. When our children respond to us in a disrespectful manner, they must be disciplined. An angry pitch, arguing, or rolling of the eyes requires correction in some form. Our job as parents is to raise thoughtful children who understand and respect authority. It's our responsibility to command respect through gentle, kind, firm, and consistent discipline.

Remember: Words speak, but examples shout. Don't waste time with your words if you're not going to follow through! Our lives must be honest representations of what we say. It is very difficult for our kids to honor our words if they feel they can't trust us. If they see

179

that we live our lives with kindness, integrity, and honor, however, they are much more likely to listen to us and engage in conversation. They know that their conversations are safe with us and that we expect truth from them, because we value truth in our own lives. As moms, we need to pray with the psalmist: "Teach me how to live, O LORD. Lead me along the path of honesty."[2]

Good Wiring, Bad Wiring

You see, proper wiring begins with us. We choose what we allow to come out of our mouths in our own homes. We can make positive choices that enhance and encourage conversation, or we can make negative choices that stifle it. The Book of Proverbs has quite a bit to say about the types of words that build relationships. When it comes to wiring for good communication, Solomon was a master electrician! As you read the following verses, note both the negative and positive ways we can communicate.[3] In fact, I encourage you to highlight the positives in one color and the negatives in another. We learn by being aware of both:

- Proverbs 4:24: "Avoid all perverse talk; stay far from corrupt speech."
- Proverbs 10:11–14: "The words of the godly lead to life; evil people cover up their harmful intentions. Hatred stirs up quarrels, but love covers all offenses. Wise words come from the lips of people with understanding, but fools will be punished with a rod. Wise people treasure knowledge, but the babbling of a fool invites trouble."
- Proverbs 10:19–21: "Don't talk too much, for it fosters sin. Be sensible and turn off the flow! The words of the godly are like sterling silver; the heart of a fool is worthless. The godly give good advice, but fools are destroyed by their lack of common sense."

- Proverbs 10:32: "The godly speak words that are helpful, but the wicked speak only what is corrupt."

- Proverbs 11:9: "Evil words destroy one's friends; wise discernment rescues the godly."

- Proverbs 11:12–13: "It is foolish to belittle a neighbor; a person with good sense remains silent. A gossip goes around revealing secrets, but those who are trustworthy can keep a confidence."

- Proverbs 11:17: "Your own soul is nourished when you are kind, but you destroy yourself when you are cruel."

- Proverbs 12:6: "The words of the wicked are like a murderous ambush, but the words of the godly save lives."

- Proverbs 12:14–19: "People can get many good things by the words they say; the work of their hands also gives them many benefits. Fools think they need no advice, but the wise listen to others. A fool is quick-tempered, but a wise person stays calm when insulted. An honest witness tells the truth; a false witness tells lies. Some people make cutting remarks, but the words of the wise bring healing. Truth stands the test of time; lies are soon exposed."

- Proverbs 12:22–23: "The LORD hates those who don't keep their word, but he delights in those who do. Wise people don't make a show of their knowledge, but fools broadcast their folly."

- Proverbs 12:25–26: "Worry weighs a person down; an encouraging word cheers a person up. The godly give good advice to their friends, the wicked lead them astray."

- Proverbs 13:1–3: "A wise child accepts a parent's discipline; a young mocker refuses to listen. Good people enjoy the positive results of their words, but those who are treacherous crave violence. Those who control their tongue will have a long life; a quick retort can ruin everything."

- Proverbs 15:1–2, 4: "A gentle answer turns away wrath, but harsh words stir up anger. The wise person makes learning a joy; fools spout only foolishness . . . Gentle words bring life and health; a deceitful tongue crushes the spirit."

- Proverbs 15:28: "The godly think before speaking; the wicked spout evil words."

- Proverbs 16:21: "The wise are known for their understanding, and instruction is appreciated if it's well presented."

- Proverbs 17:9: "Disregarding another person's faults preserves love; telling about them separates close friends."

- Proverbs 17:14: "Beginning a quarrel is like opening a floodgate, so drop the matter before a dispute breaks out."

- Proverbs 17:19: "Anyone who loves to quarrel loves sin; anyone who speaks boastfully invites disaster."

- Proverbs 17:27–28: "A truly wise person uses few words; a person with understanding is even-tempered. Even fools are thought to be wise when they keep silent; when they keep their mouths shut, they seem intelligent."

- Proverbs 18:2: "Fools have no interest in understanding; they only want to air their own opinions."

- Proverbs 18:4: "A person's words can be life-giving water; words of true wisdom are as refreshing as a bubbling brook."

- Proverbs 18:20–21: "Words satisfy the soul as food satisfies the stomach; the right words on a person's lips bring satisfaction. Those who love to talk will experience the consequences, for the tongue can kill or nourish life."

- Proverbs 21:23: "If you keep your mouth shut, you will stay out of trouble."

- Proverbs 21:28: "A false witness will be cut off, but an attentive witness will be allowed to speak."

Let's summarize what we've learned about good and bad wiring from these verses in Proverbs. Good wiring is

- Honest
- Attentive
- Kind
- Into listening more than talking
- Filled with wisdom and discernment
- Understanding
- Helpful
- Sensible
- Trustworthy
- Encouraging
- Calm, even-tempered
- Healing
- Humble
- Well-presented

Bad wiring, on the other hand, is

- Brash
- Foolish
- Inclined to talk too much
- Judgmental
- Unkind
- Angry
- Dishonest
- Cruel and destructive
- Belittling
- Prideful and overconfident
- Quick-tempered
- Overly concerned with trivial matters
- Quarrelsome

As you look over these lists, ask yourself which words or phrases characterize your communication with your family most of the time. Are there any areas that need rewiring?

Creative Conductors for Conversation

Good communication is not forced; it's enjoyed. As we seek to open up the flow of family conversation in our homes, we need to consider the most effective conductors of communication. The right timing is one. There are times when our kids are more open to talking and times when they would prefer not to talk. We can't demand conversation, but we can encourage it with good, well-timed questions and a gentle tone of voice.

When is the best time to talk? I know several families who choose breakfast time to have regular, face-to-face communication. Many other families find that conversation flows most naturally around the dinner table. For others, it is just before bed or right after the kids come home from school. Sometimes Sunday evenings offer the best time for parents and kids to be together and open up.

Another communication conductor is the right place. You don't always have to talk at home, you know. My husband and I love to take walks outside together. These are great times for chatting about the events of one another's day. Occasionally, on a particularly lovely Sunday afternoon, one of my daughters will walk with me, and we'll have a fun, leisurely conversation. Every family is different; you'll have to discover what is best for your family in terms of time and place. The dynamics may even be different with each family member. Ask the Lord to show you the best circumstances for opening up with the ones you love.

Often the best way to get discussions started is to listen to your kids and ask questions about topics that interest them. Care about what they are doing and show an interest in their friends and activities without being overly prying. What are some thoughtful questions to get everyone talking? Here are a few conversation starters:

- "Tell me something you enjoyed about today."
- "How can I pray for you this week?"
- "You played a great game today. What was your favorite moment?"
- "What did you learn from that experience?"
- "How do you feel about _____?"
- "Tell me what you think about _____."

Be careful. Conversations can end just as quickly as they started. Here are some words that will zap the life right out of good communication:

- "You always _____ (do something negative)."
- "You never _____ (do something right)."
- "I would never do what you just did."
- "Are you stupid or something?"
- "I can't believe you _____ (did something negative)."
- "What were you thinking?"

Of course, there are other good communication conductors besides conversations at the right time and place. Consider e-mailing a sweet note of encouragement to your son or daughter. Everyone loves a handwritten letter, so why not take a moment to write a note and leave it on your child's pillow? And don't think that good communication only happens one-on-one or when everyone in the room is a family member. In my home, good conversation has often erupted when our daughters' friends have come over and we've all gathered around the kitchen table to eat snacks. Open your eyes to all the potential conductors of communication in your household.

Meet your kids where they are without trying to be one of them.

By the way, in the time it has taken me to write this chapter, the cable guy has come and gone once again. This time he installed the new, up-to-date wiring. Yes, it's going to cost us a little more each month, but the clearer picture is worth the added expense. Wiring for good family communication is costly too. It costs time, patience, and an abundance of love. But the result is a clearer picture of your family, greater understanding between family members, and more peace in your home. It's well worth the expense!

Calming Thoughts

Scripture Reading: Ephesians 4:29–32; 1 Timothy 6:20; Psalm 19:14; Colossians 4:4, "Pleasant Words"

Quiet Meditations:

- What do you learn about positive conversation from these verses?
- How has the Lord convicted you about your words? What will you do differently?
- What can you do to build effective communication?

Personal Prayer:

Wonderful Father, I thank You for opening up the lines of communication with me through Your Son, Jesus. When I consider that You are the Creator of the universe, the High King of Heaven, I am amazed that You want to have a conversation with me! I confess that I often put other things in front of spending time with You. Help me to draw closer to You. Lead me and direct me in my communication with my family. Rewire me where necessary, and show me how to open the doors to positive, life-giving conversation with my husband and kids. In Jesus' name I pray, amen.

conclusion

Intimate Calm

Life is a process.
To God process isn't a means to an end; it is the goal.
Whatever sends us running to him, makes us embrace him,
causes us to depend on him, is the best good in our lives.

GLORIA GAITHER

May God bless you with his special favor and wonderful
peace as you come to know Jesus, our God and Lord, better
and better.

2 PETER 1:2 NLT

You can label me a certified zoo-aholic. I love to visit the zoo and observe God's amazing creation in the animal kingdom. My girls, on the other hand, were zooed-out by the time they were seven years old, because I insisted on dragging them to every zoo in every city we ever visited. Now that my kids have grown out of zoo-age, I'm waiting for the grandkids. We still have a few years to go!

What do you like most when you visit the zoo? Personally, I take great joy in observing the newborns: the baby chimp playing with its mother, the sweet little lamb standing next to the woolly ewe, the squealing piglets snuggling up against the big mother sow. Not too long ago a baby elephant was born at our local zoo. Watching the super-sized baby lovingly interacting with its ten-thousand-pound mother was an amazing sight!

I think the most precious scene anyone can observe is that of a mother and child, snuggled together and resting peacefully. I'm not just talking about animals. Do you remember those wonderful, peaceful moments when you held your own sleeping newborn in your arms? Could there be a more beautiful picture of calm and comfort?

Let's go a step further. Have you ever pictured yourself nestled in the divine embrace of your Heavenly Father? The Bible says, "He tends his flock like a shepherd: He gathers the lambs in his arms and carries them close to his heart; he gently leads those that have young."[1] Isn't that a wonderful picture of the tender love and care God wants to demonstrate toward us and our families? As a mom, I often feel frazzled, worried, and worn; yet when I take my cares to my Heavenly Father in prayer, I sense His loving arms wrapping gently around me, and I hear the beat of His heart.

Jesus said to His followers, "Come to me, all of you who are tired and have heavy loads, and I will give you rest. Accept my teachings and learn from me, because I am gentle and humble in spirit, and you will find rest for your lives. The teaching that I ask you to accept is easy; the load I give you to carry is light."[2] I believe Jesus is saying those same words to you and me today. We can find our rest in Him. He will provide calm in our lives. All we have to do is lay our burdens at His feet, come into His open arms, and rest in His warm embrace.

It is my hope that as you read through the chapters in this book, you felt the nudge of God's presence. Perhaps you drew closer to Him through the scriptures and prayers presented in these pages. As you move on from here toward a life of more calm and less stress, I encourage you to continue to invite God to join you each step of the way. Ask Him for His help and guidance as you seek to create a calm environment, refresh your spirit, renew your body, roll with the punches, and strengthen your family relationships. My prayer is that you will begin to know God in an ever-increasing, more personal way, accept His great love for you, and recognize His hand in the details of your life.

His Calming Presence

The story is told of an old mariner's chart that resides in a British museum. Drawn by an unknown cartographer in 1525, it charts the east coast of North America and adjacent waters and includes some peculiar markings. The original mapmaker wrote across the great areas of unexplored land and sea the following descriptions: "Here Be Giants," "Here Be Fiery Serpents," "Here Be Dragons." But at some point the chart fell into the possession and care of a scientist named John Franklin. He scratched out the fearful old markings and wrote across the map, "Here is God."[3]

What a poignant picture of the Christian life! As we place our lives in God's hands, He is able to mark out the fear and stress in our lives and replace it with His presence, His peace, and His calm. We may find ourselves in unknown territory. We may venture into uncharted waters. But we can rest assured that our loving God is with us every step of the way.

Psalm 29:11 says, "The LORD gives strength to his people; the LORD blesses his people with peace." Don't be frustrated because you don't have a perfectly calm household or a stress-free lifestyle. Peace is something that God gives. It finds its home in our hearts, not necessarily in our circumstances. The challenges we face may be stressful, but they may also be the very things that help us recognize our need for God. They may be the catalyst that causes us to seek His strength and peace and not our own.

I want to thank you for joining me on this journey to create more calm and less stress in our lives. As we part company, my hope and desire is that you and your family will benefit from the positive plan we've explored in this book. Feel free to come back and visit these pages now and then to receive encouragement and remind yourself of key points, tips, and ideas. More importantly, continue to visit God's Word. It alone holds the key to faith, hope, and the strength we need to live our lives nestled in the peace of God.

> **If you want to know more about how to have a personal relationship with Jesus, you can talk with someone right now by calling 1-800-NEED-HIM.**

Notes

Chapter 1

1. Proverbs 14:1.
2. Philippians 4:11–13.
3. Rachel St. John-Gilbert, *Wake Up Laughing* (Uhrichsville, OH: Barbour Publishing, 2004), 55–57.
4. John Cook, comp., *The Book of Positive Quotations* (Minneapolis, MN: Fairview Press, 1993), 245.
5. See Acts 13:22.
6. Psalm 37 is taken from the New Living Translation.
7. Kenneth W. Osbeck, *101 Hymn Stories* (Grand Rapids, MI: Kregel Publications, 1982), 26.

Chapter 2

1. James 1:5.
2. Colossians 3:17.
3. Proverbs 14:8 NLT.
4. Habakkuk 3:16–19 NLT.
5. Isaiah 41:10.
6. 2 Corinthians 12:9.
7. Psalm 139:23–24.
8. John 15:1, 5.
9. Roy B. Zuck, ed., *The Speaker's Quote Book* (Grand Rapids, MI: Kregel Publications, 1997), 283.

Chapter 3

1. Walter B. Knight, ed., *Knight's Master Book of Illustrations* (Grand Rapids, MI: Eerdmans Publishing Co., 1956), 755.
2. Croft M. Pentz, ed., *The Complete Book of Zingers* (Wheaton, IL: Tyndale House, 1990), 178.
3. See Matthew 6:25–33.
4. Knight, *Knight's Master Book of Illustrations*, 44.

Chapter 4

1. Pentz, *The Complete Book of Zingers*, 21.
2. Ephesians 4:26–27, 29–32.
3. Proverbs 18:4 NLT.
4. Proverbs 18:21 NLT.

Chapter 5

1. Visit the FlyLady Web site at www.flylady.net for lots of great housekeeping tips. This particular quote comes from her page "Baby Steps, Baby Steps!" at http://www.flylady.net/pages/FLYingLessons_Babysteps.asp.
2. Jennifer McMahan is a professional organizer and the owner of Space Simplicity. Her five keys are used here with her permission. Visit her Web site at www.spacesimplicity.com.

notes

3. Marcie's tips are shared with her permission. Find out more about Marcie and her ministries at www.marciehatfield.com.

Chapter 6

1. Unknown author. Copyright 2002, quotablecards.com.
2. Charles Stanley, *Finding Peace* (Nashville, TN: Thomas Nelson Publishers, 2003), 22.
3. 2 Peter 1:2.
4. John 14:27.
5. John 16:33.
6. Romans 5:1 NLT.
7. Ephesians 4:2–3.
8. Isaiah 26:3 NCV and NIV.
9. Philippians 4:7.
10. Romans 15:33 NLT.
11. Psalm 34:8.
12. Psalm 51:9–10.
13. 1 John 1:8–9.
14. Philippians 4:6–7.
15. Isaiah 26:3–4 NLT.
16. Hebrews 4:16 NLT.
17. Psalm 34:4–10 NLT.
18. Colossians 3:15.
19. James 1:2–4.
20. Sheri Prescott, *How to Be a Super Model* (Dillsboro, IN: Selah Publishing Group, 2004), 73–74.

Chapter 7

1. Adapted from Zuck, *The Speaker's Quote Book*, 423.
2. Ibid., 423.
3. Walter B. Knight, ed., *Knight's Master Book of New Illustrations* (Grand Rapids, MI: Eerdmans Publishing Co., 1994), 754–755.
4. 1 Peter 5:5–7 NET.
5. Philippians 4:6–9.
6. All verses are from the New International Version.

Chapter 8

1. John Blanchard, comp., *More Gathered Gold* (Hertfordshire, England: Evangelical Press, 1986), 23.
2. 2 Timothy 3:15–17.
3. Catherine Marshall, *A Closer Walk* (Old Tappan, NJ: Fleming Revell Co., 1986), 55–57.
4. Psalm 119:25 NLT.

Chapter 9

1. "Mood Swings," *The Doctors Book of Home Remedies for Women*, found at http://www.mothernature.com/library/bookshelf/books/19/154.cfm.

2. Gregory L. Jantz, *Moving beyond Depression* (Colorado Springs, CO: Shaw Books, 2003), 86.
3. J. Matthew Neal, "The Pituitary Gland," *Basic Endocrinology: An Interactive Approach* (Malden, MA: Blackwell Science, 2000), 21–22.
4. C. J. Johnson, "Serotonin: A Powerful Neurotransmitter," *Recipes Today*, copyright 1999–2005, iParenting, LLC, http://www.recipestoday.com/resources/articles/serotonin.htm.
5. *Random House Webster's College Dictionary*, 2nd ed., s.v. "Endorphin."
6. Randal Schober, "Endorphins: More Than a Natural High," *Imagine Your Health Magazine* (Einstein Medical, 2000), found at http://www.imagineyh.com/html/health_fitness/fitness/article/article2_sept002.php3.
7. "Mood Swings," http://www.mothernature.com/library/bookshelf/books/19/154.cfm.
8. Cyndi Schoenhals, "What Is Runner's High?" (fitFAQ.com, 2004), found at http://www.fitfaq.com/runners-high.html.
9. "Do You Live in a Blue State?" (ScoutNews LLC, copyright 2004, all rights reserved). Found on the Web site of The National Women's Health Information Center at http://www.4woman.gov/news/English/520355.htm.
10. "Mood Swings," http://www.mothernature.com/library/bookshelf/books/19/154.cfm.
11. Dr. Paul Meier of Meier Clinics recommends a liquid vitamin called To Your Health. Visit www.tyh.us for more information.
12. Johnson, "Serotonin: A Powerful Neurotransmitter," http://www.recipestoday.com/resources/articles/serotonin.htm.
13. "Mood Swings," http://www.mothernature.com/library/bookshelf/books/19/154.cfm.
14. Matthew 5:3–10 NLT.
15. Matthew 5:14–15 NLT.

Chapter 10
1. Vikki Hansen and Shawn Goodman, *The Seven Secrets of Slim People* (New York: Harper Paperbacks, 1997), 112.
2. Debra Waterhouse, *Outsmarting the Female Fat Cell* (New York: Hyperion, 1993), 128–129.
3. Charles Stuart Platkin, "Fighting Your Mood with Food" (copyright 2003 by Charles Stuart Platkin), found on the Web site of Delmarva 47 News at http://www.wmdt.com/diet/previous-diet.asp?id=40.
4. Waterhouse, *Outsmarting the Female Fat Cell*, 137.
5. John 6:35 NKJV.
6. David L. Katz, "The Way to Eat," *O, The Oprah Magazine*, September 2004, 202.

Chapter 11
1. Isaiah 55:8–9.
2. Zuck, *The Speaker's Quote Book*, 47.
3. Vernon K. McLellan, comp., *Wise Words and Quotes* (Wheaton IL: Tyndale House, 1998), 7.
4. Romans 12:2 NET.

5. Deuteronomy 31:8 NLT.
6. See Romans 8:28.
7. This story is told by Laura B. Nelson of Grapevine, Texas, and used with her permission.
8. 1 Thessalonians 5:16-18 NLT.
9. Zuck, *The Speaker's Quote Book*, 392.

Chapter 12

1. Joyce Vollmer Brown, *Courageous Christians* (Chicago, IL: Moody Press, 2000), 23–24. Story used with permission.
2. 2 Corinthians 4:16–18.
3. McLellan, *Wise Words and Quotes*, 7.
4. See Acts 22:3–4.
5. Philippians 3:13–14.
6. Luke 9:61–62.
7. *The Baptist Hymnal* (Nashville, TN: Convention Press, 1991), 406.
8. Colossians 3:1–2 NLT.

Chapter 13

1. Job 23:10–11.
2. Psalm 103:4 NIV.
3. 2 Corinthians 1:5 NIV.
4. 1 Peter 4:12–13 NLT.
5. Jill's story is used with her permission.
6. Isaiah 43:1–3.
7. Matthew 28:20.
8. James 1:2–4 NLT.
9. Job 2:10 NASB.
10. Ephesians 6:10 NKJV.
11. Romans 8:31–32.
12. 2 Corinthians 1:3–4.
13. Zuck, *The Speaker's Quote Book*, 388.

Chapter 14

1. Erma Bombeck, *Just Wait Till You Have Children of Your Own* (Brooklyn, NY: Fawcett Crest Books, 1971), 169.
2. Proverbs 31:28 NET.
3. Charles "Tremendous" Jones, ed., *Quotes Are Tremendous* (Mechanicsburg, PA: Executive Books, 1995), 41.
4. Blanchard, *More Gathered Gold*, 100.

Chapter 15

1. Genesis 2:18, 21–24 NLT.
2. Amy's story is shared with her permission.
3. Ephesians 5:31–33 NLT.
4. Psalm 27:10.
5. Romans 12:9.
6. 1 John 3:18.

7. 1 John 4:7–10.
8. If you want to learn more about the languages of love, I encourage you to read *The Five Love Languages* by Gary Chapman (Chicago, IL: Moody Press, 1992).
9. See 1 Samuel 2:19.
10. Luke 6:38–39 NLT.
11. Hebrews 12:6.
12. Psalm 103:13–14 NLT.
13. Isaiah 64:8–9 NLT.
14. Ephesians 4:2–3 NLT.

Chapter 16
1. Zuck, *The Speaker's Quote Book*, 78.
2. Psalm 27:11 NLT.
3. All of the proverbs listed here are from the New Living Translation.

Conclusion
1. Isaiah 40:11 NIV.
2. Matthew 11:28–30.
3. Knight, *Knight's Master Book of New Illustrations*, 510.

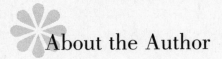

About the Author

Karol Ladd, formerly a teacher, is the author of fifteen books, including her CBA bestseller and Silver Angel Award–winning *The Power of a Positive Mom*. She is the founder and president of Positive Life Principles, Inc., and is also the cofounder of a character-building club called USA Sonshine Girls. Karol is a frequent guest on radio and television programs, sharing creative ideas for families and positive principles for life. She and her husband, Curt, have two daughters and live in Dallas, Texas.

For more information visit www.PositiveLifePrinciples.com.